MW00605633

COUGAR
FOOTBALL
COOKBOOK

COUGAR FOOTBALL COOKBOOK

Compiled by Holly Mendenhall

DESERET
BOOK

Salt Lake City, Utah

To all the Thursday's Heroes,
who inspire us every day

—Holly and Bronco

© 2013 Holly Mendenhall

All rights reserved. No part of this book may be reproduced in any form or by any means without permission in writing from the publisher, Deseret Book Company, at permissions@deseretbook.com or P. O. Box 30178, Salt Lake City, Utah 84130. This work is not an official publication of The Church of Jesus Christ of Latter-day Saints. The views expressed herein are the responsibility of the author and do not necessarily represent the position of the Church or of Deseret Book Company.

DESERET BOOK is a registered trademark of Deseret Book Company.

Visit us at DeseretBook.com

Library of Congress Cataloging-in-Publication Data
Cougar football cookbook / compiled by Holly Mendenhall.
    pages cm
  Includes index.
  ISBN 978-1-60907-015-1 (paperbound)
1. Cooking—Utah. I. Mendenhall, Holly, 1967– editor of compilation. II. Brigham Young Cougars (Football team)
  TX714.C697 2013
  642'.3—dc23   2012017078

Printed in the United States of America
Publishers Printing, Salt Lake City, UT

10   9   8   7   6   5   4   3   2   1

Contents

Water Break (Beverages)

PRE-GAME WARM-UPS

Breakfast Burritos

Laura Denney

Makes about 12 burritos

3 tablespoons extra virgin
    olive oil
1 (20-ounce) bag refrigerated
    shredded potatoes, or frozen
    hash brown potatoes
6 eggs, beaten
1 cup shredded cheddar cheese
1 cup diced ham or Canadian
    bacon
1 (15-ounce) can green chile
    sauce, such as Stokes (with
    either chicken or pork)
Salt and freshly ground pepper,
    to taste
12 uncooked flour tortillas
Salsa, if desired

Heat large skillet or stockpot over medium-high heat; cover bottom of pan with oil. Add potatoes and cook until tender, about 15 minutes, turning occasionally to ensure even browning. Add beaten eggs; scramble with potatoes. Mix in cheese, ham, and green chile sauce; season with salt and pepper to taste. Cook tortillas according to package directions; fill with approximately ½ cup egg filling. Top with a spoonful of salsa, if desired. Tuck in sides of tortillas; roll up, burrito-style.

*Laura Denney is married to **Ryan Denney, BYU defensive end from 1997 to 2001.***

Spiced Honey Butter

Sara Brown

Makes 1 cup

In small bowl, combine butter, 3 tablespoons honey, and 3 tablespoons powdered sugar. With electric mixer on low speed, add nutmeg and pumpkin pie spice. Taste for sweetness, adding additional honey and powdered sugar according to taste.

1 cup unsalted butter, softened
3–4 tablespoons honey, divided
3–6 tablespoons powdered sugar, divided
1½ teaspoons nutmeg
1–2 teaspoons pumpkin pie spice

*Sara Brown is married to **Terence Brown, BYU offensive lineman in 2005 and from 2008 to 2011.***

Whole Wheat Oatmeal Muffins

Laura Nixon

Makes 12 muffins

1 teaspoon white vinegar
1 cup milk
1 cup whole wheat flour
1 cup quick-cooking oats
⅓ cup brown sugar
1 teaspoon baking powder
½ teaspoon baking soda
½ teaspoon salt
⅓ cup oil
1 egg

Preheat oven to 425 degrees F. Mix vinegar and milk together to sour the milk (or use 1 cup buttermilk); set aside. In medium bowl, mix flour, oats, brown sugar, baking powder, baking soda, and salt. Add oil, egg, and milk mixture; stir just until blended. Fill greased muffin tins two-thirds full; bake 10 minutes.

*Laura Nixon is the mother of **David Nixon, BYU linebacker in 2003 and from 2006 to 2008.***

Pumpkin Bread

Holly Mendenhall

Makes 1 standard loaf or 4 mini loaves

Preheat oven to 350 degrees F. In medium bowl, combine flour, baking soda, baking powder, cinnamon, ginger, nutmeg, and cloves; set aside. In separate medium bowl, cream butter and sugars; stir in eggs and pumpkin. In small bowl, combine milk and vanilla; set aside. Combine flour mixture with pumpkin mixture; stir well. Stir in milk and vanilla. Pour batter into greased loaf pans. For large standard loaf, bake 1 hour; for mini loaves, bake 30 minutes.

Note: If using spiced canned pumpkin, omit spices listed above.

1½ cups flour
1 teaspoon baking soda
¼ teaspoon baking powder
1½ teaspoons cinnamon
1 teaspoon ground ginger
½ teaspoon ground nutmeg
¼ teaspoon ground cloves
6 tablespoons butter
1 cup sugar
⅓ cup brown sugar
2 eggs
1 cup pumpkin
⅓ cup milk
½ teaspoon vanilla

*Holly Mendenhall is married to **Coach Bronco Mendenhall, BYU head coach since 2005.***

Easy Chocolate Chip Banana Bread

Brooke PoVey Howell

Makes 1 loaf

1½ cups flour
1 cup sugar, or less
1 teaspoon baking soda
½ teaspoon salt
¼ cup vegetable oil
3 bananas, mashed
2 eggs, lightly beaten
1 cup chocolate chips

Preheat oven to 350 degrees F. Grease and flour 8½ x 4½-inch loaf pan (or spray pan with floured baking spray). In large bowl, whisk together flour, sugar, baking soda, and salt; mix in oil, bananas, and eggs. Stir in chocolate chips, but do not over-mix. Pour into prepared pan; bake until toothpick inserted in center comes out clean, about 70 to 80 minutes. Cool loaf in pan 10 minutes; turn out and cool completely, right side up.

*Brooke PoVey Howell is married to **Nick Howell, BYU defensive backs coach and special team coordinator since 2008.***

Homemade Granola Bars

Brooke PoVey Howell

Makes 14 bars

Preheat oven to 350 degrees F.; generously grease 9 x 13-inch baking pan. In large bowl, mix together oats, brown sugar, wheat germ, flaxseed, cinnamon, flour, sesame seeds, raisins, chocolate chips, almonds, and salt. Make a well in center of mixture; add honey, egg, oil, and vanilla and almond extracts. Mix well, using hands if necessary. Pat mixture evenly into prepared pan. Bake 12 to 15 minutes, or until bars begin to turn golden at edges; do not overcook. Cool 5 minutes; cut into bars while still warm (bars will be hard to cut if allowed to cool completely before cutting).

2 cups old-fashioned rolled oats

¾ cup packed brown sugar

½ cup wheat germ

¼ cup ground flaxseed

1 teaspoon cinnamon

1 cup whole wheat flour

Sesame seeds, optional

¾ cup raisins, optional

2 cups semisweet chocolate chips, optional

½ cup slivered almonds, optional

¾ teaspoon salt

½ cup honey

1 egg, beaten

½ cup vegetable oil

2 teaspoons vanilla extract

1 teaspoon almond extract

*Brooke PoVey Howell is married to **Nick Howell, BYU defensive backs coach and special team coordinator since 2008.***

Fire and Ice Salsa

Breanna Nielsen

Makes 3 cups

3 cups seeded and chopped
　　watermelon
½ cup chopped green peppers
2 tablespoons lime juice
1 tablespoon chopped cilantro
1 tablespoon chopped green
　　onion
2 tablespoons chopped jalapeño
　　peppers
Tortilla chips

In medium bowl, combine all ingredients; mix well and cover. Refrigerate at least 1 hour. Serve with warm tortilla chips.

*Breanna Nielsen is married to **Austin Nielsen, BYU offensive lineman in 2006 and from 2009 to 2011.***

Becca's Salsa

Becca Eason

Makes 12 servings

1 (28-ounce) can diced or
   stewed tomatoes
2 (14.5-ounce) cans tomatoes,
   such as Ro*Tel
½ cup diced onions
⅓ cup chopped cilantro
1½ teaspoons garlic salt
1 teaspoon ground cumin
½ teaspoon sugar

Blend all ingredients in blender. For best results, refrigerate at least 12 hours.

*Becca Eason is married to **Corby Eason, BYU defensive back from 2009 to 2011.***

Game Day Fresh Guacamole

Brooke PoVey Howell

Makes 8 to 10 servings

10–12 small to medium ripe
  avocados
1 large tomato, chopped
1 medium yellow onion,
  chopped
1 bunch fresh cilantro, chopped
Juice of 1 lemon
Juice of 1 lime
Salt, to taste
Chips or sliced vegetables

Peel avocados; place in large bowl. Mash with potato masher just until lumpy; do not overmash. Mix in tomato, onion, and cilantro; add lemon and lime juices and salt to taste. Chill before serving; serve within an hour of preparation or guacamole will turn brown. Serve with chips, such as whole wheat pita chips, or sliced vegetables.

Brooke PoVey Howell is married to **Nick Howell, BYU defensive backs coach and special team coordinator since 2008.**

Stuffed Mushrooms

Sara Brown

Makes 11 to 12 mushrooms

2 (8-ounce) packages fresh
    button mushrooms
1 (16-ounce) package country-
    style sausage
1 (8-ounce) package cream
    cheese, softened

Preheat oven to 400 degrees F. Wipe or rinse off mushrooms and remove stems. Place mushroom caps on baking sheet; set aside. In large skillet over medium heat, cook sausage until browned; drain fat. Transfer cooked sausage to medium bowl. Stir in cream cheese; mix well. Spoon mixture into mushroom caps; bake 30 to 45 minutes, depending on size of caps.

*Sara Brown is married to **Terence Brown, BYU offensive lineman in 2005 and from 2008 to 2011.***

O-Line Poppers

Sara Brown

Makes 30 poppers

15 jalapeño peppers
2 (8-ounce) packages cream
    cheese (low-fat cream cheese
    may be used), softened
1 (12-ounce) package bacon or
    turkey bacon

Preheat oven to 400 degrees F. Wash jalapeños; put on food preparation gloves and cut stems from jalapeños. Cut jalapeños lengthwise and scrape out seeds and veins (the white part that holds the seeds—and most of the heat). On foil-lined baking sheet, place jalapeños skin side down. Place softened cream cheese in zip-top bag; seal and cut off a corner of the bag. Fill jalapeño halves with cream cheese. Cut bacon strips in half lengthwise; wrap each jalapeño with a piece of bacon. Bake 20 minutes; cool. Serve alone or with salsa.

Note: Because oils in hot peppers may irritate skin, food preparation gloves are recommended when working with hot peppers. Avoid touching eyes or mouth while handling peppers.

*Sara Brown is married to **Terence Brown, BYU offensive lineman in 2005 and from 2008 to 2011.***

Gyoza (Pot Stickers)

Tina Frazier

Makes about 100 dumplings

¼ head of cabbage

1–2 carrots

3 cloves garlic

1 pound ground beef (uncooked)

2 teaspoons soy sauce

2 teaspoons sesame oil

6 drops ra–yu (hot chili oil)

¼ teaspoon salt

¼ teaspoon pepper

1–2 packages round gyoza or
wonton wrappers (about 50
wrappers per package)

Vegetable oil

Chop cabbage, carrots, and garlic in food processor; mix well with ground beef. Season with soy sauce, sesame oil, ra–yu, salt, and pepper. Moisten edge of gyoza wrapper; place a small spoonful of filling in center. Fold gyoza in half and pleat top edge, sealing it to moistened flat edge. To heated skillet, add 1 tablespoon vegetable oil and 6 to 8 gyoza; lightly brown bottom of wrappers. Add ¼ cup water to skillet; cover immediately and steam pot stickers 1 minute. Repeat process until all filling has been used.

*Tina Frazier is married to **Jameson Frazier, BYU linebacker from 2008 to 2011.***

Jalapeño Crescent Rolls

Breanna Nielsen

Makes 8 rolls

1 (8-ounce) can crescent roll
   dough
2 ounces cream cheese
2 slices pepper Jack cheese
¼ cup canned jalapeño
   peppers, minced

Preheat oven to 375 degrees F. Separate crescent rolls into individual triangles; place on ungreased cookie sheet. Spread cream cheese along short edge of crescent roll. Place ¼ slice pepper Jack cheese over cream cheese. Scatter minced jalapeño along length of crescent roll; roll up. Bake 11 to 13 minutes.

*Breanna Nielsen is married to **Austin Nielsen, BYU offensive lineman in 2006 and from 2009 to 2011.***

Preheat oven to 350 degrees F. In medium bowl, combine Gruyère, cream cheese, garlic, chives, mayonnaise, Tabasco sauce, salt, and pepper; mix well and adjust flavors. Squeeze excess water from crab before adding; add crab, if desired. Mix well; set aside. Spread butter on baguettes; bake until lightly browned. Place a spoonful of cheese mixture on each slice; bake 10 to 15 minutes, until cheese starts to brown. Garnish with chopped chives and serve.

To roast garlic: Place cloves in nonstick sauté pan on medium heat, with no oil. Toss for about 15 minutes, until heavy brown freckles appear on cloves.

Gruyère Crostini
Rory Rauschenbach

Makes 6 to 8 servings

1½ cups grated Gruyère cheese

1 (8-ounce) package cream cheese, softened

6–7 cloves garlic, roasted, minced

1 tablespoon finely chopped chives or green onions, plus more for garnish

½ cup mayonnaise

Dash Tabasco sauce

Salt and pepper, to taste

1 (5-ounce) can crab, well drained, picked clean, and chopped, optional

20 baguette slices, ½-inch thick

Butter for baguette

Rory Rauschenbach was a BYU linebacker from 1975 to 1978.

Apache Cheese Bread

Holly Mendenhall

Makes 12 servings

1 (9-inch) round loaf hard bread
16 ounces sharp cheddar
    cheese, shredded
1 (8-ounce) package cream
    cheese, softened
1 (8-ounce) carton sour cream
½ cup chopped green onions
1 teaspoon Worcestershire sauce
2 (4.5-ounce) cans chopped
    green chiles
1 cup chopped ham
Chips or French bread

Preheat oven to 350 degrees F. Cut top of bread off horizontally; save top. Scoop out inside of loaf; set aside. Combine all ingredients; mix well (mixture will be stiff). Fill bread shell with cheese mixture; replace top. Place on cookie sheet; bake 1 hour 10 minutes. Cube bread from inside of loaf and use for dipping, or serve cheese mixture with chips or small pieces of French bread.

*Holly Mendenhall is married to **Coach Bronco Mendenhall, BYU head coach since 2005.***

Asian Grilled Chicken Salad

Kelly Rhea

Makes 3–4 servings

1 (10.7-ounce) package Dole
   Asian Island Crunch Salad Kit
¼ cup pineapple juice
1 tablespoon soy sauce
1 teaspoon brown sugar, packed
1 clove garlic, finely chopped
2 (8-ounce) boneless, skinless
   chicken breasts
1 cup thinly sliced red bell
   pepper
¼ cup thinly sliced Dole red
   onion

In small saucepan, combine 1 tablespoon sesame ginger dressing from salad kit with pineapple juice, soy sauce, brown sugar, and garlic. Bring to boil and reduce liquid to ⅓. Brush chicken breasts with dressing mixture. Heat grill or grill pan over medium-high heat; brush lightly with oil or spray with non-stick vegetable cooking spray. Grill chicken, turning once, 10 to 12 minutes, or until no longer pink in center, basting frequently. Slice chicken. In large bowl, place salad blend from kit with accompaniments provided; toss with remaining dressing. Arrange salad on plates; top with bell pepper, onion, and chicken.

*Kelly Rhea is married to **Jeff Rhea, BYU offensive lineman from 2001 to 2002 and from 2005 to 2007.***

Steak and Spinach Salad

Samantha Workman Kariya

Makes 8 to 10 servings

Grill steak to medium-rare; slice into thin strips. Place steak strips in container; pour marinade over strips. Cover; marinate 3 to 24 hours in refrigerator. When ready to serve, drain excess marinade. In salad bowl, toss together marinated steak strips, oranges, strawberries, and spinach; serve.

For marinade: Combine all ingredients in blender; process until smooth.

1 pound flank steak

2 (11-ounce) cans mandarin or fresh oranges

1 pint strawberries

1 (16-ounce) package baby spinach

Marinade

1½ cups salad oil

3 tablespoons poppy seeds

1¼ cups sugar

2 teaspoons dry mustard

2 teaspoons salt

⅔ cup white vinegar

4 tablespoons grated onion

*Samantha Workman Kariya is married to **Bryan Kariya, BYU running back from 2008 to 2011.***

Wild Rice Salad with Artichoke Hearts

Brooke PoVey Howell

Makes 4 servings

1 (6-ounce) package long grain
  and wild rice mix
1 tablespoon minced onion
½ cup diced celery
¼ cup diced green pepper
1 (6–8-ounce) jar artichoke
  hearts, drained and cut up
1–2 cups salad shrimp, or
  cooked cubed chicken
½ cup mayonnaise
2 tablespoons olive oil
2 tablespoons lemon juice
½ teaspoon curry, optional
1 teaspoon freshly minced
  parsley or 1 tablespoon
  dehydrated parsley
Salt and pepper, to taste

Cook rice according to package directions; drain and cool. Add remaining ingredients; combine well. Refrigerate if not serving immediately.

*Brooke PoVey Howell is married to **Nick Howell, BYU defensive backs coach and special team coordinator since 2008.***

Spinach Salad with Poppy Seed Dressing

Lenore V. Mendenhall

Makes 4 to 5 servings

Combine spinach, bacon, onion, Swiss cheese, Craisins, and candied almonds. Pour poppy seed dressing over salad; serve immediately.

For candied almonds: In saucepan over medium-high heat, place ½ cup sugar and almonds; stir until sugar begins to melt and brown (watch closely—almonds may burn quickly). Remove from heat; spread on cutting board or baking sheet to cool. When cool, break into small pieces.

For dressing: Mix together sugar, mustard, and vinegar. Microwave at high power 30 seconds to dissolve sugar; mix well. Stir in oil, poppy seeds, and onion salt; mix again.

1 (9-ounce) bag spinach
¼ pound bacon, cooked and crumbled
1 red onion, minced
2 cups Swiss cheese
2 cups Craisins

Candied Almonds
½ cup sugar
2 cups almonds

Poppy Seed Dressing
¾ cup sugar
1 teaspoon dry mustard
⅓ cup red wine vinegar
1 cup olive oil
1 tablespoon poppy seeds
1⅓ teaspoons onion salt

*Lenore V. Mendenhall is the mother of **Coach Bronco Mendenhall, BYU head coach since 2005.***

BLT Salad

Kelly Rhea

Makes 4 servings

⅓ cup extra virgin olive oil,
    divided
6 slices thick-cut bacon,
    chopped
1 clove garlic, grated, or
    crushed and minced
1 tablespoon Dijon mustard
2 tablespoons white balsamic
    vinegar or white wine
    vinegar
Salt, to taste
Freshly ground black pepper,
    to taste
3 tablespoons chives, chopped
2 hearts of romaine lettuce
1 pint multi-colored, red or
    yellow cherry tomatoes

Into medium skillet, drizzle 1 tablespoon extra virgin olive oil; heat over medium–high. Add bacon; cook until crisp. Drain on paper-towel-lined plate. In salad bowl, whisk together garlic, mustard, and vinegar; stream in remaining extra virgin olive oil. Season with salt and pepper to taste; stir in chives. Shred hearts of romaine; add to dressing in bowl. Cut cherry tomatoes in half; add tomatoes and bacon to salad in bowl. Toss until salad is evenly coated with dressing; serve immediately.

*Kelly Rhea is married to **Jeff Rhea, BYU offensive lineman from 2001 to 2002 and from 2005 to 2007.***

Avocado Grapefruit Salad

Sallie Stephens

Makes 8 servings

Break lettuce apart; place equal portions on eight plates. Arrange avocados, grapefruit, oranges, bananas, and kiwi on top of lettuce.

For dressing: Combine all ingredients; drizzle over prepared salads.

1 head iceberg lettuce, washed and drained

2 ripe avocados, sliced

2 large grapefruit, peeled and sectioned

1 (15-ounce) can mandarin oranges, drained

2 bananas, sliced

2 large kiwi, peeled and sliced

Dressing

⅓ cup sugar

1 teaspoon dry mustard

1 teaspoon paprika

1 teaspoon celery seed

¼ cup white vinegar

1 cup canola oil

*Sallie Stephens is married to **Brandon Stephens, BYU offensive lineman in 1997 and from 2000 to 2003.***

Pear and Walnut Salad

Kris Anne Gustavson

Makes 8 servings

¼ cup walnuts

1 head romaine lettuce, torn
  into pieces

1 (12-ounce) package mixed
  greens

2 pears, unpeeled, sliced

½ pound feta cheese, crumbled

¼ pound cooked bacon,
  crumbled, optional

Dressing

1 cup sugar

1 teaspoon salt

½ small onion, chopped

1 teaspoon dry mustard

¾ cup canola oil

½ cup white vinegar

1 teaspoon poppy seeds

Preheat oven to 350 degrees F. Roast walnuts on baking sheet 10 to 15 minutes; allow to cool. When walnuts are cool, mix with lettuce, greens, pears, feta, and bacon.

For dressing: Blend ingredients thoroughly; chill. Being careful not to saturate salad, slowly pour dressing over salad. Pour a small amount, stir, taste, and add more dressing as needed.

*Kris Anne Gustavson is married to **Paul Gustavson, BYU center in 1973**.*

Sweet and Sour Dressing

Holly Mendenhall

Makes 1 pint

Mix together vinegar and sugar; microwave at high power 20 seconds or until sugar is dissolved. Add remaining ingredients; mix well. Dressing keeps well in refrigerator in covered container.

½ cup apple cider vinegar

½ cup sugar

1 cup olive oil

Dash Tabasco sauce

2 teaspoons salt

⅛ teaspoon lemon pepper

*Holly Mendenhall is married to **Coach Bronco Mendenhall, BYU head coach since 2005.***

BOWL GAMES

Tomato Basil Soup

Kelly Rhea

Makes 12 to 16 servings

2 tablespoons butter, melted
6 large carrots, chopped
1½ white onions, chopped
3 (14-ounce) cans stewed
    tomatoes
2 quarts chicken broth
1 (32-ounce) can tomato purée
1 tablespoon dried basil
2 cups fat-free half-and-half
Salt, to taste
Pepper, to taste
Parmesan cheese

Melt butter in large soup pot; sauté carrots and onions until soft. Add remaining ingredients, except Parmesan cheese; heat thoroughly. Cool mixture thoroughly in refrigerator; purée in batches in blender. (If mixture is not thoroughly cooled, steam will blow the lid off the blender.) Adjust salt and pepper to taste. To make cheese crisps for soup toppers, place heaping tablespoons of shredded Parmesan cheese on baking sheet; broil until crispy, about 5 minutes.

*Kelly Rhea is married to **Jeff Rhea, BYU offensive lineman from 2001 to 2002 and from 2005 to 2007.***

Ginger Squash Soup

Vicki Omer

Makes 4 to 6 servings

½ cup chopped onion
6 cups peeled, seeded, and
    chopped butternut squash
2 tablespoons minced ginger
2 (10.75-ounce) cans condensed
    chicken or vegetable broth
4 cloves garlic
2–3 tablespoons fresh lime juice
Salt and pepper, to taste

In large soup pot, combine onion, squash, and ginger; add broth and garlic, and bring to a boil. Reduce heat and simmer 5 minutes, until squash is tender. Fill blender or food processor about one-third full of squash mixture; process until smooth. Continue to blend mixture in batches until all is processed. Return mixture to pot; stir in lime juice, salt, and pepper. To thin soup, add water, a tablespoon at a time.

*Vicki Omer is married to **Coach Jay Omer, BYU head strength and conditioning coach since 2000;** she is also the mother of **Joe Omer, BYU wide receiver from 2001 to 2003.***

Gold Soup

Vicki Omer

Makes 6 servings

1 medium onion, chopped

4–5 medium carrots, cut in
    chunks

2 ribs celery, chopped

2 medium potatoes, peeled if
    desired, and diced

1 clove garlic, minced

4 cups chicken or vegetable
    broth

1 cup milk or evaporated milk

4 tablespoons butter

Salt and pepper, to taste

In large pot, combine onion, carrots, celery, potatoes, garlic, and broth; bring to a boil. Cover and reduce to low; simmer 20 to 30 minutes, or until potatoes and carrots are tender. Fill blender or food processor about one-third full of vegetable mixture; vent lid to prevent steam buildup and process until smooth. Process soup in batches, and then strain puréed soup as it is poured back into pot. Stir in milk and butter until butter is melted; heat through, but do not boil. Season with salt and pepper to taste.

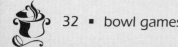

*Vicki Omer is married to **Coach Jay Omer, BYU head strength and conditioning coach since 2000;** she is also the mother of **Joe Omer, BYU wide receiver from 2001 to 2003.***

Clam Chowder

Samantha Workman Kariya

Makes 16 servings

4 (6.5-ounce) cans minced clams
1–2 large onions, finely chopped
3–4 ribs celery, chopped
5–6 russet potatoes, peeled and
  cubed
1½ cups water
1 to 1½ cups butter
1½ cups flour
2 quarts half-and-half
2 teaspoons salt
1 teaspoon pepper
3 bay leaves
2 teaspoons Italian seasoning

Drain clams, reserving juice. In large soup pot, pour clam juice over vegetables; add water to cover. Simmer until vegetables are tender, about 15 minutes. Meanwhile, in separate large stockpot, melt butter; stir in flour, cooking and stirring constantly until smooth. Add half–and–half and spices; heat through, but do not boil. Add clams and vegetables; adjust spices to taste. Remove bay leaves before serving.

*Samantha Workman Kariya is married to **Bryan Kariya, BYU running back from 2008 to 2011.***

Chicken Noodle Soup

Sara Brown

Makes 8 to 10 servings

3 carrots, peeled and diced
3 ribs celery, diced
1 medium onion, diced
2 tablespoons butter or
    margarine
6 cups chicken broth
6 cups water
2 cups shredded cooked
    chicken breast
3 teaspoons chicken bouillon,
    to taste
Salt and pepper, to taste
2 tablespoons parsley flakes
½ (8-ounce) package acine di
    pepe pasta

In stockpot over medium heat, sauté carrots, celery, and onion in melted butter, stirring frequently, until softened. Stir in chicken broth and water; increase heat to medium-high, and bring mixture to a boil. Stir in shredded chicken; simmer 10 minutes. Add bouillon to taste; season with salt, pepper, and parsley. Stir in pasta; cook until pasta is soft.

*Sara Brown is married to **Terence Brown, BYU offensive lineman in 2005 and from 2008 to 2011.***

Dave's Bean Soup

Laura Nixon

Makes 16 servings

Soak beans overnight according to package directions; save seasoning packet for another use. In slow cooker, cook beans, tomatoes, onion, and garlic 8 hours on low heat setting. Purée mixture in blender or food processor; add olive oil and salt to taste. Serve with freshly squeezed lemon or lime juice, grated Parmesan cheese, and tortilla chips.

1 (20-ounce) package 10- or 15-bean soup
1 (14.5-ounce) can diced tomatoes, such as Ro*Tel
1 onion, chopped
4 cloves garlic, minced
¼ to ½ cup olive oil, to taste
Salt, to taste
Freshly squeezed lemon or lime juice, to taste
Grated Parmesan cheese, for garnish
Tortilla chips, for garnish

*Laura Nixon is the mother of **David Nixon, BYU linebacker in 2003 and from 2006 to 2008.***

Taco Soup

Breanna Nielsen

Makes 4 to 6 servings

1 pound ground beef
1 small onion, chopped
2½ cups chunky salsa
1 (15-ounce) can kidney beans, drained
1 (28-ounce) can diced tomatoes, undrained
1 (15.25-ounce) can whole kernel corn, undrained
1 teaspoon chili powder
½ teaspoon garlic powder
1 (1.25-ounce) package taco seasoning mix
½ cup shredded cheddar cheese, optional, for garnish
½ cup sour cream, optional, for garnish
Tortilla chips, optional, for garnish

In large saucepan, brown ground beef and onion together until meat is no longer pink and onion is translucent; drain fat and place mixture in large slow cooker. Add remaining ingredients, except for garnishes, and stir to combine; cook 3 hours on low heat setting, until well heated and flavors are blended. Serve in bowls and garnish with cheese, sour cream, and tortilla chips as desired.

*Breanna Nielsen is married to **Austin Nielsen, BYU offensive lineman in 2006 and from 2009 to 2011.***

Chicken Taco Soup

Kristy Denney

Makes 8 servings

In slow cooker, combine onion, beans, corn, tomato sauce, diced tomatoes, and taco seasoning; top with chicken breasts, pressing down to allow other ingredients to cover chicken. Cook 5 hours on low heat setting; remove chicken from soup and shred. Stir shredded chicken back into soup; cook 2 hours more. Serve with sour cream, shredded cheese, and crushed tortilla chips, if desired.

1 medium onion, chopped
1 (15-ounce) can chili beans, undrained
1 (15-ounce) can black beans, undrained
1 (15.25-ounce) can whole kernel corn, drained
1 (8-ounce) can tomato sauce
2 (10-ounce) cans diced tomatoes with green chiles
1 (1.25-ounce) package taco seasoning mix
3 whole boneless, skinless chicken breasts
Sour cream, optional
Shredded cheddar cheese, optional
Tortilla chips, optional

*Kristy Denney is married to **Brett Denney, BYU defensive lineman in 2003 and from 2006 to 2009.***

Mary's Hungry Man Chunky Butternut Chili

Mary Jolley

Serves 6 hungry men (or 8 hungry women)

1 medium onion, chopped
3 tablespoons canola oil
4 cloves garlic, diced
2 teaspoons ground cumin
1 teaspoon crushed red pepper
1 teaspoon paprika
½ teaspoon salt
¼ teaspoon freshly ground
    black pepper
2 red bell peppers, roasted
2 cups vegetable broth or water
1½ cups peeled, cubed butternut
    squash (about ½-inch cubes)
1 (15-ounce) can white beans,
    rinsed and drained
1 (15-ounce) can kidney beans,
    rinsed and drained
1 (28-ounce) can diced tomatoes,
    undrained
Sliced green onions, optional
Diced avocado, optional
Tortilla chips, optional
Shredded cheddar cheese, optional

In large, heavy pot over medium heat, sauté onions in oil 10 minutes, or until onions are soft and translucent. Stir in garlic, cumin, crushed red pepper, paprika, salt, and pepper. Add roasted red bell peppers, broth or water, squash, beans, and tomatoes; simmer, covered, 25 to 30 minutes, until stew thickens and squash is soft. Serve with green onions, avocado, tortilla chips, and cheese, if desired.

To roast red bell peppers: Cut peppers in half lengthwise; remove seeds and white membrane. Place pepper halves, skin side up, on baking sheet; broil 15 to 20 minutes. Remove from baking sheet and seal in zip-top bag 15 minutes. Remove peppers from bag; pull off and discard skin. Chop peppers into ⅓-inch pieces; set aside.

38 • bowl games

*Mary Jolley is married to **Doug Jolley, BYU tight end from 1997 to 2001.***

Laura's Butternut Squash Chili

Laura Denney

Makes 6 servings

Heat stockpot or Dutch oven over medium heat. Sauté onion in oil 15 minutes, stirring occasionally. Add cumin, red pepper flakes, paprika, salt, and garlic; cook and stir 2 minutes more. Add roasted bell peppers, vegetable broth, squash, and tomatoes; simmer 20 minutes, stirring occasionally. Add beans; simmer 20 to 30 minutes more, stirring occasionally. Season with freshly ground pepper, to taste. Serve with garnishes, if desired.

To roast red bell peppers: Preheat broiler. On foil-lined baking sheet, broil bell peppers 20 minutes, or until blackened. Remove peppers from baking sheet and seal in zip-top plastic bag 15 minutes. Cut peppers in half lengthwise, discarding stem and seeds. Peel and chop peppers.

Note: To cube a whole, raw butternut squash, peel squash, and then cut it in half, scoop out seeds, and chop squash into cubes.

1 medium onion, chopped
3 tablespoons extra virgin olive oil
2 teaspoons ground cumin
½ teaspoon crushed red pepper
1 teaspoon paprika
½ teaspoon salt
4 garlic cloves, finely chopped
2 red bell peppers, roasted
2 cups vegetable broth
2 cups peeled, cubed butternut squash (½-inch cubes)
2 (14.5-ounce) cans diced tomatoes, undrained, or 2 cups diced fresh tomatoes
1 (15-ounce) can pinto beans, drained and rinsed
1 (15-ounce) can cannellini beans, drained and rinsed
1 (15-ounce) can red kidney beans, drained and rinsed
Freshly ground pepper
½ cup thinly sliced green onions, for garnish
½ cup shredded cheddar cheese, for garnish
1 avocado, diced, for garnish
1 small bunch cilantro, chopped, for garnish

Laura Denney is married to **Ryan Denney, BYU defensive end from 1997 to 2001.**

Wendy's Slow-Cooked Sweet Potato Chili

Wendy Nielsen

Makes 6 to 8 servings

1 (28-ounce) can crushed tomatoes
1 (14.5-ounce) can diced tomatoes
2 tablespoons chili powder
1 tablespoon ground cumin
2 teaspoons smoked paprika
1 tablespoon brown sugar
½ teaspoon salt
2 large sweet potatoes, peeled and
    chopped into 1-inch pieces
1 medium onion, coarsely chopped
2 cloves garlic, minced
1 (15-ounce) can kidney beans,
    drained if desired
1 (15-ounce) can black beans,
    drained if desired
1 pound ground sirloin (browned if
    desired), optional

In slow cooker, combine ingredients, stirring well. Cook 10 hours on low heat setting.

*Wendy Nielsen is married to **Gifford Nielsen, BYU quarterback from 1975 to 1977.***

Fiery Habañero Chili

Vicki Omer

Makes 8 servings

In large soup pot, cook bacon over medium-high heat until evenly browned. Remove bacon; drain on paper towels. Drain excess bacon fat from pot, leaving enough to coat bottom of pot. Chop bacon; set aside. In pot over medium-high heat, brown beef and pork. When meat is browned, stir in remaining ingredients, except beans and reserved bacon. Reduce heat to low; simmer 45 to 60 minutes, stirring occasionally. Add beans and bacon; simmer 30 minutes more.

½ pound bacon
1 pound ground beef
1 pound ground pork
1 green bell pepper, diced
1 yellow onion, diced
6 jalapeño peppers, seeded and chopped
6 habañero peppers, seeded and chopped
8 Anaheim peppers, seeded and diced
2 cloves garlic, minced
1½ tablespoons ground cumin
1 tablespoon crushed red pepper flakes
3 tablespoons chili powder
2 tablespoons beef bouillon granules
1 (28-ounce) can crushed tomatoes
2 (14.5-ounce) cans whole peeled tomatoes, drained
1½ cups apple juice
1½ tablespoons tomato paste
1 teaspoon chile paste
2 cups water
2–4 (15-ounce) cans chili beans, drained

*Vicki Omer is married to **Coach Jay Omer, BYU head strength and conditioning coach since 2000;** she is also the mother of **Joe Omer, BYU wide receiver from 2001 to 2003.***

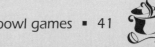

Game Day Stew

Pat Edwards

Makes 25 servings

2–3 pounds stew meat
2 tablespoons olive oil
4–6 carrots, diced
4–6 potatoes, diced
2 (1-ounce) packages dried soup
    mix, such as Lipton's Onion
1 (26-ounce) can cream of
    mushroom soup
1 (10.75-ounce) can condensed
    cream of mushroom soup
1 teaspoon salt
½ teaspoon pepper
½ to 1 cup water

Preheat oven to 225 to 300 degrees F. Brown stew meat in oil. Add remaining ingredients, except water; mix together. Bake 5 to 6 hours in heavy, covered, cast-iron pan; add water, as needed, for desired consistency.

*Pat Edwards is married to **LaVell Edwards, BYU head coach from 1972 to 2000.***

Green Chile Chicken Stew

Makes 6 servings

In 4-quart Dutch oven with cover, heat oil; add chicken and cook until lightly browned. Stir in onion and garlic; add flour and stir 1 to 2 minutes. Add tomatoes, green chiles, jalapeño, salt, pepper, and sugar; mix well. Stir in broth; lower heat. Cover pot; simmer 1½ hours, or until meat is tender. Serve with flour tortillas.

2 tablespoons olive oil

2 pounds chicken breast, cut into 1-inch cubes

½ cup chopped onion

1 clove garlic, minced

¼ cup flour

2 cups peeled, chopped fresh tomatoes

3 (4-ounce) cans diced green chiles, drained

1 fresh jalapeño pepper, chopped

1 teaspoon salt

½ teaspoon ground black pepper

½ teaspoon sugar

1 cup chicken broth

Flour tortillas

*Holly Mendenhall is married to **Coach Bronco Mendenhall, BYU head coach since 2005.***

bowl games ▪ 43

TOUCHDOWN!

Chicken Rollups

McKenzie Mendenhall

Makes 16 rollups

4–6 boneless, skinless chicken
 breasts
1 (8-ounce) package cream
 cheese, softened
1 teaspoon poultry seasoning
2 (4-ounce) cans diced green
 chiles
2 (8-ounce) cans crescent roll
 dough, such as Pillsbury
¼ cup butter, melted
1 cup crushed, uncooked stuffing
 mix, such as Stove Top
Chicken gravy

Cook chicken; shred. Into cream cheese, mix poultry seasoning and green chiles. Mix cheese mixture with shredded chicken. Divide crescent rolls into individual triangles; place on lightly greased baking sheet. Place a spoonful of chicken mixture in center of each triangle and roll up. Lightly brush with melted butter; top with crushed stuffing mix. Bake according to directions for rolls; serve with chicken gravy.

*McKenzie Mendenhall is married to **Zeke Mendenhall, BYU linebacker from 2009 to 2010.***

Swiss Cheese Chicken

Becca Eason

Makes 5 servings

Place chicken breasts in slow cooker; top with Swiss cheese slices. In small bowl, combine butter, milk, and soup; spread mixture over Swiss cheese. Top with stuffing mix. Cook 6 to 8 hours on low heat setting or 4 to 6 hours on high.

5 chicken breast halves

10 slices Swiss cheese

½ cup butter, melted

¼ cup milk

1 (10.75-ounce) can condensed cream of mushroom soup

1 (6-ounce) box chicken-flavored stuffing mix, such as Stove Top

*Becca Eason is married to **Corby Eason, BYU defensive back from 2009 to 2011.***

Catalina Cranberry Chicken

Orrin Olsen

Makes 8 to 12 servings

8–10 chicken breast halves
1 (16-ounce) can whole
   cranberry sauce
1 (1-ounce) envelope dry onion
   soup mix
1 (16-ounce) bottle Catalina
   dressing

Preheat oven to 350 degrees F. Place chicken in 9 x 13-inch pan. Mix together cranberry sauce, soup mix, and dressing; pour mixture over chicken. Bake 1 hour, uncovered.

Orrin Olsen was a BYU defensive end and offensive center from 1971 to 1975.

Chicken Tetrazzini

Laura Nixon

Makes 8 to 10 servings

Preheat oven to 350 degrees F. Sauté green pepper in oil; remove from pan. In separate pan, melt butter or margarine over low heat; blend in flour. Add milk and ½ cup chicken broth; stir over medium heat, until thick. Add sautéed green pepper, mushroom soup, grated cheese, mushrooms, and pimiento; stir until cheese is melted. Add chopped chicken. Cook pasta in chicken broth (add water if necessary) until tender but still firm (al dente), 7 to 10 minutes; drain. Stir sauce mixture into pasta; place in greased 9 x 13-inch baking pan. Bake until hot and bubbly, about 20 to 25 minutes.

1 green bell pepper, diced
2 tablespoons vegetable oil
¼ cup butter or margarine
5 tablespoons flour
1 cup milk
6–8 cups chicken broth (from cooking chicken), divided
1 (10.75-ounce) can condensed cream of mushroom soup
½ pound sharp cheddar cheese, grated
1 (10.75-ounce) can mushrooms
1 (4-ounce) jar chopped pimiento
3 cups chopped cooked chicken
8 ounces vermicelli or thin spaghetti noodles

*Laura Nixon is the mother of **David Nixon, BYU linebacker in 2003 and from 2006 to 2008.***

Buffalo Chicken Macaroni and Cheese

Christy Denney

Makes approximately 8 servings

- 1 pound elbow macaroni
- 7 tablespoons unsalted butter, divided
- 1 small onion, finely chopped
- 2 ribs celery, finely chopped
- 3 cups shredded rotisserie chicken
- 2 cloves garlic, minced
- ¾ cup buffalo wing sauce, such as Frank's, divided
- 2 tablespoons flour
- 2 teaspoons dry mustard
- 2½ cups half-and-half
- 1 pound yellow sharp cheddar cheese, cut into 1-inch cubes (about 3½ cups)
- 8 ounces pepper Jack cheese, shredded (about 2 cups)
- ⅔ cup sour cream
- 1 cup panko bread crumbs
- ½ cup crumbled bleu cheese
- 2 tablespoons chopped fresh parsley

Preheat oven to 350 degrees F.; spray 9 x 13-inch baking dish with cooking spray. Bring large pot of salted water to a boil. Add macaroni and cook until tender but still firm (al dente), about 7 minutes; drain. While macaroni is cooking, melt 3 tablespoons butter in large skillet over medium heat. Add onion and celery; cook until soft, about 5 minutes. Stir in chicken and garlic; cook 2 minutes more. Add ½ cup buffalo wing sauce; simmer until slightly thickened, about 1 minute. In separate saucepan over medium heat, melt 2 tablespoons butter; stir in flour and mustard until smooth. Whisk in half-and-half and remaining ¼ cup wing sauce; cook and stir until thick, about 2 minutes. Whisk in cheddar and pepper Jack cheeses; whisk in sour cream until smooth. Combine chicken mixture and cooked macaroni; toss with cheese sauce to coat well. Pour into prepared baking dish. In microwave-safe dish, microwave remaining 2 tablespoons butter until melted; stir in panko crumbs, bleu cheese, and parsley. Sprinkle crumb mixture over macaroni; bake 30 to 40 minutes, or until bubbly. Let stand 10 minutes before serving. Best if served immediately.

*Christy Denney is married to **John Denney, BYU defensive end and long snapper from 2001 to 2004.***

Ena's Famous Chicken

Michele Lewis

Makes 5–6 servings

In large bowl, combine soy sauce, water, brown sugar, garlic, and onions; pour over chicken thighs to completely cover. Marinate 2 to 24 hours in refrigerator. Grill on medium heat, about 8 minutes each side.

1 cup soy sauce

1 cup water

1 cup brown sugar

1 heaping teaspoon crushed
    garlic

5–6 green onions, chopped

10–12 boneless, skinless chicken
    thighs

*Michele Lewis is married to **Chad Lewis, BYU tight end from 1993 to 1996.***

Chicken, Beans, and Cream Cheese

Monica DuPaix

Makes 16 servings

4 chicken breasts
2 (15-ounce) cans black beans,
    undrained
1 (15.25-ounce) can whole
    kernel corn, drained, or
    10 ounces frozen corn
1 (16-ounce) jar salsa (mango
    with peach salsa is
    recommended)
2 cloves garlic, crushed
1 (8-ounce) package cream
    cheese
Cooked rice or corn chips, such
    as Fritos

Place chicken in slow cooker; cover with beans, corn, salsa, and garlic. Cover and cook 7 to 8 hours on low heat setting, or until chicken is tender. If desired, remove chicken from cooker and shred (chicken will shred more easily the longer it is cooked); place chicken back in cooker. Add cream cheese; stir until cream cheese melts. Cook one more hour; serve over rice or corn chips.

Note: This is a great gluten-free dish.

*Monica DuPaix is married to **Coach Joe DuPaix, BYU running backs coach and recruiting coordinator since 2001.***

Pistachio Basil Butter Salmon

Brooke PoVey Howell

Makes 4 servings

In blender, combine all ingredients, except salmon; process until smooth. Spread a generous amount of pistachio butter on top of grilled salmon; allow butter to melt. Serve with brown or wild rice, salad, or steamed vegetables.

Note: Pistachio butter is excellent on other fish and chicken.

¼ cup pistachios

10 fresh basil leaves

1 clove garlic

½ cup butter, room temperature

1 teaspoon lime juice

Salt and pepper, to taste

4 hot grilled salmon fillets

*Brooke PoVey Howell is married to **Nick Howell, BYU defensive backs coach and special team coordinator since 2008.***

Salmon Dijon

Rory Rauschenbach

Makes 8 servings

2 cups mayonnaise
2 tablespoons Dijon mustard
Juice of ½ medium lemon
½ teaspoon Tabasco sauce
1 tablespoon dried dill weed
2 tablespoons pickle juice
2 tablespoons half-and-half
8 (6–7-ounce) salmon fillets

Preheat oven to 350 degrees F. In large mixing bowl, mix together all ingredients, except salmon, until smooth; coat salmon fillets well with sauce. Place fillets on baking sheet; bake 15 to 20 minutes, or until golden-brown spots begin to appear on salmon. Remove from oven; let stand a few minutes before serving.

Rory Rauschenbach was a BYU linebacker from 1975 to 1978.

Strawberry Pork Chops

Samantha Workman Kariya

Makes 4 servings

Preheat oven to 375 degrees F. Season pork chops with salt and pepper. In medium bowl, toss strawberries with basil and balsamic vinegar; let stand 15 to 20 minutes. Heat oven-proof skillet over medium-high; add oil and sear pork chops 2 to 3 minutes. Place pan in oven; roast pork chops 10 to 12 minutes. Cool 5 minutes; top with strawberries.

4 (1½-inch thick) boneless pork chops
Pinch salt
Pinch pepper
2 cups fresh sliced strawberries
1 cup shredded fresh basil
¼ cup aged balsamic vinegar
2 tablespoons virgin olive oil

*Samantha Workman Kariya is married to **Bryan Kariya, BYU running back from 2008 to 2011.***

Slow-Cooked Pork Chops, Cabbage, and Apples

Sara Brown

Makes 4 servings

4 boneless pork chops
Salt, to taste
Pepper, to taste
½ cup applesauce
2 apples, peeled and chopped
Dash nutmeg
Dash cinnamon
1 head cabbage (core removed),
    chopped
¼ cup chicken broth

Season pork chops with salt and pepper; place in slow cooker. Cover with applesauce and apples; sprinkle with nutmeg and cinnamon. Add cabbage; pour chicken broth over all. Cook 4 hours on high heat setting or 6 to 8 hours on low.

*Sara Brown is married to **Terence Brown, BYU offensive lineman in 2005 and from 2008 to 2011.***

Oven Kalua Pig

Kris Anne Gustavson

Makes 10 servings

2 tablespoons salt

2 tablespoons Accent seasoning

¼ cup soy sauce

1 teaspoon Worcestershire sauce

1 teaspoon garlic salt

1 (5-pound) pork roast

3 teaspoons liquid smoke

Preheat oven to 375 degrees F. In small bowl, mix together salt, Accent seasoning, soy sauce, Worcestershire sauce, and garlic salt; rub pork roast thoroughly with seasoning mixture. Place roast on large piece of foil, pour liquid smoke over roast, and wrap in foil. Place in roasting pan; roast 5 hours.

*Kris Anne Gustavson is married to **Paul Gustavson, BYU center in 1973.***

Best-Ever Barbecue Sauce

Sandy Olsen

Makes 2 to 2½ cups

1 cup ketchup
½ teaspoon pepper
1 tablespoon butter
¼ cup sugar
2 tablespoons white vinegar
¾ cup water or roast drippings
1 teaspoon dry mustard
1 teaspoon celery salt
1 teaspoon paprika
1 teaspoon Worcestershire sauce
½ onion, chopped
3 pounds ground beef, cooked,
   or shredded roast beef

In 2-quart saucepan, simmer all ingredients 15 to 20 minutes. Pour over cooked ground beef or shredded roast beef; simmer on low heat.

Note: Sauce is also excellent with whole or shredded chicken or with spareribs.

*Sandy Olsen is married to **Orrin Olsen, BYU defensive end and offensive center from 1971 to 1975.***

Cornish Pasties (pass-tees)

Melanie Hunsaker

Makes 8 pasties

Preheat oven to 350 degrees F. Divide pie crust pastry into 8 pieces and roll into flat circles. In large mixing bowl, combine ground beef, hash browns, dried onions, soup, and carrots. Place approximately ¾ cup meat mixture on each piece of pastry; fold in half and pinch edges together. In small bowl, combine egg and milk; brush over pasties. Bake 1 hour; serve with brown gravy, if desired.

Pastry for 2-crust pie
2 pounds ground beef
4 cups frozen hash brown
    potatoes, thawed
¼ to ½ cup dried onions,
    to taste
1 (10.75-ounce) can condensed
    cream of mushroom soup
½ cup sliced carrots
1 egg
¼ cup milk

*Melanie Hunsaker is married to **Burke Hunsaker, BYU wide receiver in 1993.***

The Best Italian Meatballs

Brianna Reynolds

Makes about 24 meatballs

1 ¼ pounds ground beef

2 teaspoons Worcestershire
   sauce

1 beaten egg

½ cup Italian bread crumbs

¼ cup grated Parmesan cheese

2 cloves garlic, chopped

Salt, to taste

Pepper, to taste

Preheat oven to 425 degrees F. Combine all ingredients well. Roll into 1-inch balls; place on ungreased baking sheet. Bake 10 to 15 minutes.

*Brianna Reynolds is married to **Matt Reynolds, BYU offensive lineman from 2007 to 2011.***

Slow-Cooked Turkey Spinach Lasagna

Brooke PoVey Howell

Makes 8 servings

In large skillet over medium heat, sauté onion, garlic, and ground turkey in oil until turkey is no longer pink; drain fat. In large bowl, combine turkey, marinara sauce, and tomatoes. In separate bowl, mix ricotta cheese, 1 cup mozzarella cheese, salt, and oregano. Coat large slow cooker with cooking spray; pour 1 cup turkey-tomato mixture into cooker. Layer ⅓ each of noodles, ricotta mixture, mozzarella, and ½ of spinach. Repeat layers, starting with sauce, and using remaining spinach in second layer. Layer a third time in the following order: sauce, noodles, ricotta, mozzarella, sauce; top with Italian-blend cheese. Cover; cook 2½ to 3 hours on low heat setting, or until noodles are soft and cheese is melted. Sprinkle with grated Parmesan cheese.

1 large onion
1 teaspoon minced garlic
½ pound ground turkey
1 tablespoon olive oil
1 (26-ounce) jar marinara sauce
1 (14.5-ounce) can diced tomatoes
3 cups part-skim ricotta cheese
1 (10-ounce) package shredded part-skim mozzarella cheese, divided
½ teaspoon salt
1½ tablespoons oregano
1 (9-ounce) package oven-ready whole wheat lasagna noodles, uncooked
1 (10-ounce) package frozen, chopped spinach, thawed and squeezed, or 6 cups fresh spinach
2 cups shredded Italian-blend cheese
6 tablespoons grated Parmesan cheese

Brooke PoVey Howell is married to **Nick Howell, BYU defensive backs coach and special team coordinator since 2008.**

Lasagna Rollups

Breanna Nielsen

Makes 6 to 8 servings

1½ pounds ground beef

1 onion, chopped

2 cloves garlic, minced

1 (26-ounce) jar spaghetti sauce

2 teaspoons brown sugar

¼ teaspoon salt

½ teaspoon pepper

1 (8-ounce) package cream
    cheese, softened

½ cup butter, softened

2 cups small curd cottage
    cheese, room temperature

1 egg

1 (16-ounce) package lasagna
    noodles

1 (8-ounce) package shredded
    mozzarella cheese

2 tablespoons Parmesan cheese

In large saucepan over medium heat, cook ground beef, onion, and garlic until meat is browned; drain fat. Stir in spaghetti sauce, brown sugar, salt, and pepper. Cover; cook 2 hours on low heat setting. Preheat oven to 350 degrees F. Coat 9 x 13-inch pan with cooking spray. Combine cream cheese, butter, cottage cheese, and egg until smooth; set aside. Cook lasagna noodles according to package directions; drain. Spread a large spoonful of cheese filling the length of 1 cooked lasagna noodle; roll up and place in pan. Repeat with remaining noodles and filling. When pan is full, top with shredded mozzarella and Parmesan cheese; cover with meat sauce. Bake 30 minutes.

*Breanna Nielsen is married to **Austin Nielsen, BYU offensive lineman in 2006 and from 2009 to 2011.***

Four-Cheese Baked Penne

Sydney Leung-Wai

Makes 8 servings

Heat oven to 400 degrees F. In medium bowl, combine cottage cheese, ½ cup mozzarella, ricotta cheese, and parsley. Cook pasta until tender but still firm (al dente); drain. In large pot over medium heat, heat oil; sauté onion, stirring occasionally, 5 minutes. Add garlic; cook, stirring, 30 seconds more. Stir in tomatoes, tomato sauce, oregano, rosemary, salt, pepper flakes, and pepper; bring to a boil. Reduce heat; simmer until sauce thickens slightly, about 10 minutes. Add pasta; remove from heat. Stir in cheese-parsley mixture. Coat 9 x 13-inch glass baking dish with cooking spray; transfer pasta mixture to dish. Top with remaining ¾ cup mozzarella and Parmesan cheese; bake until heated through and cheese melts, about 30 minutes.

1½ cups small curd low-fat cottage cheese

1¼ cups shredded part-skim mozzarella cheese, divided

1 cup part-skim ricotta cheese

3 tablespoons chopped fresh parsley

1 pound whole wheat penne

2 teaspoons olive oil

1 medium onion, chopped

4 cloves garlic, chopped

1 (14.5-ounce) can crushed tomatoes

1 (8-ounce) can no-salt-added tomato sauce

1 teaspoon dried oregano

1 teaspoon dried rosemary

¾ teaspoon salt

½ teaspoon red pepper flakes

¼ teaspoon freshly ground black pepper

¼ cup shredded Parmesan cheese

*Sydney Leung-Wai is married to **Aveni Leung-Wai, BYU linebacker from 2010 to 2011.***

Stromboli

Sallie Stephens

Makes 8 servings

1 (16-ounce) loaf frozen bread
　　dough, thawed

1 cup (4 ounces) shredded
　　mozzarella cheese

¼ pound sliced pepperoni,
　　Canadian bacon, or other
　　meat of choice

3 ounces sliced provolone
　　cheese

¼ pound thinly sliced ham, or
　　other meat or vegetable
　　topping of choice

1 tablespoon melted butter

1 (14-ounce) jar pizza sauce

Preheat oven to 375 degrees F. Place bread dough on lightly greased baking sheet; pat to 15 x 10-inch rectangle. Arrange mozzarella cheese lengthwise down center of rectangle; top with layers of pepperoni and provolone cheese, and then ham. Moisten edges of dough with water. Fold long edges of dough to center; press edges together securely to seal. Seal ends; brush loaf with melted butter. Bake on greased baking sheet 20 minutes, or until lightly browned. Cool on wire rack; slice with electric knife. Serve with pizza sauce for dipping.

*Sallie Stephens is married to **Brandon Stephens, BYU offensive lineman from 1997 to 2000.***

Pasta Rustica

Kimberly Jacobson

Makes 6 to 8 servings

Preheat oven to 350 degrees F. In large Dutch oven over medium heat, heat olive oil; sauté onion until golden, about 5 minutes. Add garlic; cook, stirring, 1 minute. Add ground beef; cook until no longer pink, about 6 minutes. Stir in basil, oregano, and red pepper flakes; sprinkle with Italian seasoning. Add tomatoes and reserved purée; bring to a boil. Reduce heat to medium-low; simmer, stirring occasionally, until thickened, about 10 to 12 minutes. Fill large soup pot three-fourths full of water; bring to a boil over high heat. Add salt and pasta; stir well. Cook until pasta is barely tender but still firm (al dente), 10 to 12 minutes; drain well. In large bowl, toss pasta with sauce, ricotta, and mozzarella. Spread in ungreased 9 x 13-inch pan; sprinkle with Parmigiano-Reggiano cheese. Bake 30 minutes, or until cheeses are melted and pasta is browned. Let stand 5 minutes before serving.

2 tablespoons olive oil

1 yellow onion, chopped

2 garlic cloves, minced

¾ pound ground beef

1 teaspoon dried basil

1 teaspoon dried oregano

¼ teaspoon hot red pepper flakes

½ teaspoon Italian seasoning

1 (28-ounce) can tomatoes in purée, tomatoes coarsely chopped and purée reserved

Salt, to taste

1 pound penne pasta

1¼ cups ricotta cheese

2 cups shredded mozzarella cheese

½ cup grated Parmigiano-Reggiano cheese

*Kimberly Jacobson is married to **McKay Jacobson, BYU wide receiver in 2006 and from 2009 to 2011.***

Creamy Tomato Basil Pasta

Amanda Ogletree

Makes approximately 4 servings

3 cups bow tie pasta

1 tablespoon minced garlic

⅓ cup olive oil

1 (14.5-ounce) can diced
  tomatoes, undrained

1 tablespoon dried basil

¾ tablespoon chicken bouillon

1 cup cream

½ cup grated Parmesan cheese

Fresh basil, for garnish, optional

Cook pasta according to package directions; drain and set aside. In saucepan on medium-low heat, sauté garlic in oil, about 2 minutes. Add diced tomatoes, basil, and chicken bouillon; cook about 5 minutes. Add cream; simmer until sauce reaches desired thickness. Add Parmesan cheese, stirring as it melts, about 1 to 2 minutes. Serve over pasta; garnish with fresh basil.

Note: This pasta is excellent with grilled chicken.

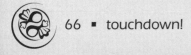

*Amanda Ogletree is married to **Brandon Ogletree, BYU linebacker from 2008 to 2012.***

Veggie Fajitas

Mary Jolley

Makes 6 fajitas

Heat oil in large skillet over medium heat; add onion, red pepper, mushrooms, and garlic. Cook until softened, about 10 to 15 minutes. Add cumin, chili powder, and ½ of lime juice; season with salt and pepper to taste. Cook 3 minutes. Increase heat to medium-high; add chopped tomatoes, and cook 2 to 3 minutes. Remove from heat. In small bowl, mash avocados with remaining lime juice and ½ teaspoon salt; set aside. Heat pinto beans and corn. In dry pan over medium heat, heat tortillas until warmed. Place 1 tortilla on flat surface. Place a scoop of pinto beans down center of tortilla; top with a scoop of cooked mixture and a strip each of corn, avocado, and lettuce. Tuck in sides of tortillas; roll up, burrito-style.

1 tablespoon canola oil

1 small onion, cut into thin slices

1 red bell pepper, cut into thin slices

9–10 white button mushrooms, thinly sliced

1 clove garlic, minced

1 teaspoon ground cumin

½ teaspoon chili powder

Juice of 1 lime, divided

½ teaspoon salt, plus more for seasoning, to taste

Freshly ground black pepper, to taste

2 tomatoes, chopped

2 avocados

6 whole wheat tortillas

1 (15-ounce) can pinto beans, rinsed and drained

1 (15.25-ounce) can whole kernel corn, drained

1 cup romaine lettuce, shredded or cut in very thin strips

*Mary Jolley is married to **Doug Jolley, BYU tight end from 1997 to 2001.***

touchdown! ▪ 67

Veggie Pizza

Sara Brown

Makes 4 to 6 servings

2 (8-ounce) cans crescent roll
    dough
1 (8-ounce) package onion and
    chive cream cheese
¼ to ½ cup each of raw
    vegetables, such as
    mushrooms, green onions,
    tomatoes, carrots, broccoli

Spray baking sheet with cooking spray. Place crescent roll dough on cookie sheet; seal edges and flatten. Bake according to package directions. Cool; spread with cream cheese. Top with vegetables; cut into slices and serve.

*Sara Brown is married to **Terence Brown, BYU offensive lineman in 2005 and from 2008 to 2011.***

Hummus Bagel Sandwich

Mary Jolley

Makes 1 serving

Slice bagel in half horizontally; toast. Spread each side of bagel with hummus; sprinkle with salt, pepper, and sunflower seeds. On one half of bagel, layer cucumber slices; add carrot, banana peppers, and sprouts. Top with other half of bagel.

1 whole-grain bagel
¼ cup hummus, plain or seasoned
Pinch salt
Freshly ground black pepper, to taste
2 teaspoons raw sunflower seeds
5 slices cucumber
2 tablespoons shredded carrot
5 mild bottled banana pepper slices
⅓ cup alfalfa sprouts

*Mary Jolley is married to **Doug Jolley, BYU tight end from 1997 to 2001.***

Dinner Rolls

Sara Brown

Makes 36 rolls

½ cup warm water

½ cup plus 1 teaspoon sugar, divided

4 teaspoons yeast

2 cups warm milk

7 cups white flour, divided

3 eggs

4 tablespoons melted butter

1½ teaspoons salt

Stir together warm water and 1 teaspoon sugar; add yeast. Let sit 5 minutes until foamy. Mix together ½ cup sugar, milk, and yeast mixture. Stir in 3 cups flour; mix well. Add eggs, butter, and salt; mix thoroughly with mixer or by hand. Stir in remaining flour; place dough in greased bowl. Spray top of dough with nonstick cooking spray; let rise 1 hour or until doubled in size. On floured surface, roll dough into a 12 x 12-inch square. Cut into 36 2 x 2-inch squares; place squares on greased baking sheet. Let rise 30 minutes or until doubled; bake 10 to 12 minutes at 350 degrees F.

Variation: To make orange rolls, brush ¼ cup melted butter on rolled-out dough. Sprinkle dough with zest from 2 oranges and ½ cup sugar; cut into squares. Roll each square into a small spiral; let rise until doubled. Bake 2 to 4 minutes longer than dinner rolls. After rolls are cooled, mix together ½ cup powdered sugar, 1 tablespoon orange zest, and 3 to 4 tablespoons orange juice (thin with additional water or orange juice, as needed); drizzle over rolls.

*Sara Brown is married to **Terence Brown, BYU offensive lineman in 2005 and from 2008 to 2011.***

Kassie's Pani Popo (Coconut Buns)

Kassie Feinga

Makes 12 servings

Mix together coconut milk, flour, and sugar; pour in bottom of greased 9 x 13-inch cake pan. Place frozen dinner rolls on top of mixture. Let rise 4 to 5 hours, or according to package directions. Preheat oven to 350 degrees F.; bake rolls 10 to 15 minutes, or until golden brown. Serve either warm or cooled.

1 (14-ounce) can coconut milk
¼ cup flour
½ cup sugar
12 packaged frozen dinner rolls,
    such as Rhodes

*Kassie Feinga is married to **Ray Feinga, BYU offensive lineman from 2004 to 2008.***

McKenzie's Coconut Rolls

McKenzie Mendenhall

Makes 12 servings

12 bake-and-serve rolls, such as
    Rhodes
1 (14-ounce) can coconut milk
1 cup sugar

On greased baking sheet, place rolls one inch apart; let rise according to package directions. When rolls have risen, preheat oven to 350 degrees F. In medium pan, warm coconut milk and sugar together over low heat until sugar dissolves. Pour milk-and-sugar mixture over rolls; bake 15 minutes, until slightly browned.

*McKenzie Mendenhall is married to **Zeke Mendenhall, BYU linebacker from 2009 to 2010.***

Cheddar Bay Biscuits

Christy Denney

Makes 12 biscuits

Preheat oven to 400 degrees F. Lightly grease baking sheet or line with parchment paper; set aside. In medium bowl, using pastry cutter or two forks, combine baking mix with cold butter until chunks of butter are the size of peas. Stir in cheddar cheese, milk, and garlic powder just until combined; do not overmix. Drop by ¼-cup portions onto prepared baking sheet; bake 13 to 15 minutes, until tops of biscuits begin to turn light brown.

For glaze: While biscuits are baking, melt butter in small bowl in microwave; stir in garlic powder and parsley flakes. Brush garlic butter on tops of baked biscuits; sprinkle with kosher salt.

2½ cups baking mix, such as Bisquick
4 tablespoons cold butter
1 cup shredded cheddar cheese
¾ cup milk
¼ teaspoon garlic powder

Butter Glaze
3 tablespoons butter
½ teaspoon garlic powder
¾ teaspoon dried parsley flakes
Kosher salt

*Christy Denney is married to **John Denney, BYU defensive end and long snapper from 2001 to 2004.***

Twice-Baked Ranch Potatoes

Anna Beck Staffieri

Makes 4 to 6 servings

3 medium to large russet
   potatoes
2 strips bacon
¾ cup ranch salad dressing
1 teaspoon salt
1 teaspoon pepper
1 cup Mexican-blend shredded
   cheese

Preheat oven to 400 degrees F. Scrub potatoes; bake 1 hour in oven or microwave until soft (leftover baked potatoes may also be used). Cool. Fry bacon until slightly undercooked. Remove bacon from pan and chop; set aside. Cut cooled potatoes in half lengthwise. Using small spoon, scoop out insides of potatoes into medium bowl, leaving skins intact; set skins aside. To potatoes in bowl, add ranch salad dressing, salt, and pepper; blend until creamy. Scoop potato mixture into potato skins; place on oven-safe pan. Top each potato half with chopped bacon and plenty of shredded cheese. Bake until cheese melts and begins to bubble, about 15 to 20 minutes for room-temperature potatoes, or longer if potatoes have been refrigerated.

*Anna Beck Staffieri is married to **Markell Staffieri, BYU linebacker in 2001 and from 2004 to 2007;** she is also the sister of **John Beck, BYU quarterback from 2003 to 2006.***

Creamed Potatoes and Peas

Sara Brown

Makes 4 servings

Dice potatoes; boil in water until not quite fork-tender. If needed, add enough water to barely cover potatoes; add peas and cook until soft. Drain, reserving liquid. In small bowl, mix a slurry of ½ to 1 cup cooking liquid, milk, and cornstarch. Add slurry to potato and pea mixture; cook and stir 5 minutes over medium heat. Stir in butter, salt, and pepper to taste.

3 medium russet potatoes, unpeeled, scrubbed
1 cup frozen peas
2 tablespoons milk
2–3 tablespoons cornstarch
3 tablespoons butter
Salt and pepper, to taste

*Sara Brown is married to **Terence Brown, BYU offensive lineman in 2005 and from 2008 to 2011.***

Baked Carrots and Potatoes

Monica DuPaix

Makes 12 to 15 servings

¼ cup olive oil

3 tablespoons lemon juice

¾ teaspoon garlic powder

½ teaspoon onion powder

1 teaspoon oregano

1 teaspoon salt

½ teaspoon pepper

4 cups baby carrots

6–8 red potatoes, unpeeled,
    each cut into about 8 pieces

Preheat oven to 450 degrees F. In small bowl, mix together oil, lemon juice, garlic powder, onion powder, oregano, salt, and pepper. Place carrots and potatoes in large casserole dish. Pour seasoning mixture over potatoes and carrots; stir until vegetables are well coated. Bake 1 hour.

*Monica DuPaix is married to **Coach Joe DuPaix, BYU running backs coach and recruiting coordinator since 2011.***

Mashed Sweet Potatoes

Sara Brown

Makes 4 to 6 servings

Boil whole sweet potatoes 30 to 40 minutes, until fork-tender. Cool; slip skins off. Chop sweet potatoes into medium-sized pieces; add salt, pepper, butter, and cream. Mash sweet potatoes; add honey and cayenne, to taste.

3–4 large sweet potatoes
Salt and pepper, to taste
3 tablespoons butter, softened
⅛ cup cream or half-and-half
3 tablespoons honey
Pinch cayenne pepper, or more,
    to taste

*Sara Brown is married to **Terence Brown, BYU offensive lineman in 2005 and from 2008 to 2011.***

Squash Casserole

Sara Brown

Makes 6 to 8 servings

6–8 medium zucchini, yellow
squash, or grey squash
1¼ cups sour cream
4 tablespoons butter
2 cups shredded cheddar
cheese, divided
Salt and pepper, to taste
10–12 butter crackers, such as
Ritz

Preheat oven to 350 degrees F. Cut squash into 1-inch pieces; boil in water until soft, and then drain thoroughly. Place squash in 9 x 9-inch buttered baking dish; mix in sour cream and butter. Stir in 1½ cups cheese; add salt and pepper, to taste. Spread mixture evenly in dish; top with crumbled butter crackers and remaining cheese. Bake 30 to 40 minutes.

*Sara Brown is married to **Terence Brown, BYU offensive lineman in 2005 and from 2008 to 2011.***

Pineapple Bake

Lenore V. Mendenhall

Makes 8 servings

¾ cup butter

¾ cup sugar

¾ cup brown sugar

2 eggs

1 (20-ounce) can chunk
   or crushed pineapple,
   undrained

½ cup half-and-half

Pinch salt

2 cups fresh white bread cubes

Cream butter and sugars. Add eggs; beat until smooth. Stir in pineapple until well mixed. Add half-and-half, salt, and bread cubes; stir until blended. Pour into 9 x 13-inch baking dish; bake 1 hour at 350 degrees F. Serve warm.

Note: This dish is excellent with ham, pork, or lamb.

*Lenore V. Mendenhall is the mother of **Coach Bronco Mendenhall, BYU head coach since 2005.***

Pine Nut Sage Stuffing

Rory Rauschenbach

Makes 8 servings

2 loaves white bread
1 large onion, chopped
6 ribs celery, chopped
½ cup olive oil
6 cloves garlic, minced
2 (14.5-ounce) cans chicken
    stock, divided (add more,
    according to taste)
½ cup butter
1 tablespoon dried sage
1 cup pine nuts
3 whole eggs, beaten
12 leaves fresh sage
Salt and pepper, to taste

Cut bread into small cubes; let dry at room temperature, or toast bread cubes in roasting pan at 350 degrees F. (watch carefully and turn cubes often). In large skillet, sauté onion and celery in olive oil about 8 minutes. Add garlic; sauté 2 minutes. Deglaze pan by stirring in ¼ cup chicken stock and scraping bottom of pan to blend in browned, flavorful bits of onion, celery, and garlic. Add butter and dried sage; melt butter slowly. Add bread cubes; toss gently until all cubes are coated. Add nuts, remaining stock, eggs, and fresh sage; mix thoroughly to desired consistency. Add salt and pepper to taste. Stuff bird with dressing or bake dressing 20 to 25 minutes at 350 degrees F.

Rory Rauschenbach was a BYU linebacker from 1975 to 1978.

Coconut Lime Rice

Vicki Omer

Makes 6 servings

1½ cups brown rice
1 (14-ounce) can coconut milk
¼ cup water
3 tablespoons chopped fresh
   mint, optional
1 lime, zested and juiced

Rice cooker (makes 3 cups rice): Cook rice according to rice cooker directions, using coconut milk and ¼ cup water, approximately 1½ to 2 hours. Blend in mint, lime zest, and lime juice. If instant rice is used, adjust amounts of coconut milk and water according to package directions.

Stove top (makes 2 cups rice): To 1 can coconut milk, add water to equal 1½ cups; pour into pot or pan with tight-fitting lid, and bring to a boil. Stir 1 cup brown rice into boiling mixture. Cover with lid, and reduce heat to low. Simmer at least 50 minutes without lifting lid. After 50 minutes, lift lid and test to see if rice is soft and liquid is absorbed. If not, let rice sit, covered, approximately 10 minutes more.

Blend mint, lime zest, and lime juice into cooked rice.

*Vicki Omer is married to **Coach Jay Omer, BYU head strength and conditioning coach since 2000;** she is also the mother of **Joe Omer, BYU wide receiver from 2001 to 2003.***

Luau Rice

Kris Anne Gustavson

Makes 10 servings

2 cups uncooked white rice (not
 instant)
2 cups chicken broth
3 cups water
2 onions, diced
1 cup butter, cubed

Preheat oven to 400 degrees F. Mix all ingredients together; place in greased 9 x 13-inch or similar baking dish. Bake, uncovered, 1 hour.

*Kris Anne Gustavson is married to **Paul Gustavson, BYU center in 1973.***

Brown Sugar Spice Cake

Breanna Nielsen

Makes 8 servings

1 (10.75-ounce) can condensed
   tomato soup
½ cup water
2 eggs
1 (15.25-ounce) package spice
   cake mix
1¼ cups hot water
¾ cup packed brown sugar
1 teaspoon ground cinnamon
Vanilla ice cream

Spray inside of 3½- to 4-quart slow cooker with cooking spray. Mix soup, water, eggs, and cake mix; pour into cooker. In small bowl, stir together hot water, brown sugar, and cinnamon; pour over cake batter. Cover; cook on high heat setting 2 to 2½ hours, or until toothpick inserted in center comes out clean. Spoon cake into bowls; top with sauce from bottom of cooker. Serve with vanilla ice cream.

*Breanna Nielsen is married to **Austin Nielsen, BYU offensive lineman in 2006 and from 2009 to 2011.***

Fresh Apple Cake

Laura Nixon

Makes 12 servings

Preheat oven to 350 degrees F. Beat eggs 1 minute; add sugars and oil. In separate bowl, sift together flour, baking soda, salt, and spices. Mix dry ingredients into wet ingredients; add vanilla. With wooden spoon, stir in apples and nuts; batter will be very stiff. Spray Bundt pan with nonstick cooking spray; pour in cake mixture. Bake 1 hour 15 minutes.

2 eggs

2 cups sugar

½ cup packed brown sugar

1 ½ cups vegetable oil

3 cups flour

1 ½ teaspoons baking soda

1 teaspoon salt

1 teaspoon cinnamon

Dash nutmeg

1 teaspoon vanilla

3 cups chopped apples

1 cup chopped pecans or walnuts

*Laura Nixon is the mother of **David Nixon, BYU linebacker in 2003 and from 2006 to 2008.***

Strawberry Chocolate Chip Shortcake

Sallie Stephens

Makes 12 servings

1 cup sugar, divided

½ cup butter or margarine, softened

3 eggs, divided

2 teaspoons vanilla extract, divided

1½ cups flour

½ teaspoon baking powder

1 cup miniature semisweet chocolate chips, divided

2 cups sour cream

2 cups frozen nondairy whipped topping, thawed

Fresh strawberries, stemmed, washed, and halved

Preheat oven to 350 degrees F.; grease 9-inch springform pan. In large bowl, beat ½ cup sugar and butter. Add 1 egg and 1 teaspoon vanilla; beat until creamy. Gradually add flour and baking powder, beating until smooth; stir in ½ cup miniature chocolate chips. Press mixture onto bottom of prepared pan. In medium bowl, stir together sour cream, remaining ½ cup sugar, remaining 2 eggs, and remaining 1 teaspoon vanilla; stir in remaining ½ cup miniature chocolate chips. Pour over mixture in pan; bake 50 to 55 minutes, until almost set in center and edges are lightly browned. Cool completely on wire rack; remove sides of pan. Spread whipped topping over top of cake; cover and refrigerate. Just before serving, arrange strawberry halves on top of cake; garnish as desired. Refrigerate leftover dessert.

*Sallie Stephens is married to **Brandon Stephens, BYU offensive lineman in 1997 and from 2000 to 2003.***

Chocolate Chip Cake

Pat Edwards

Makes 8 servings

1 (18.25-ounce) package yellow cake mix, such as Duncan Hines

1 package (4-serving size) instant chocolate pudding mix

½ cup sugar

¾ cup canola oil

¾ cup water

4 eggs

1 cup sour cream

¾ cup chocolate chips

Preheat oven to 350 degrees F. Mix together cake mix, pudding mix, and sugar; stir in oil and water. Add eggs one at a time; beat with wooden spoon after each addition. Stir in sour cream and chocolate chips; pour batter into greased and floured Bundt pan. Bake 50 to 60 minutes; cool one hour before removing from pan.

This recipe was given to me by Cindy Meyer, the wife of Ron Meyer, who was head coach of Southern Methodist University (SMU) when BYU beat them in the Miracle Bowl. Cindy and I were good friends, and I knew how badly she must have felt after the game. I wrote to her and told her that I knew the loss was hard on her but that friendship is more important than a football game. She agreed that friendship is to be valued, and to prove it she sent me this wonderful cake. I make this cake every game day.

Pat Edwards is married to **LaVell Edwards, BYU head coach from 1972 to 2000.**

Chocolate Mousse Cake

Melanie Hunsaker

Makes 12 servings

2 cups sugar
2 cups flour
1 package (4-serving size) instant
    chocolate pudding mix
¾ cup cocoa
1½ teaspoons baking soda
1½ teaspoons baking powder
½ teaspoon salt
2 eggs
1 cup milk
½ cup oil or softened margarine
2 teaspoons vanilla
¾ cup boiling water

Preheat oven to 350 degrees F. Grease and flour 2 round 9-inch cake pans. In large mixing bowl, combine sugar, flour, pudding mix, cocoa, baking soda, baking powder, and salt. Add eggs, milk, oil or margarine, and vanilla; beat 2 minutes on medium speed. Add boiling water; mix well. Pour into pans; bake 30 to 35 minutes. Cool cake 10 minutes and remove from pans; cool completely. After cakes are cooled, place bottom cake layer in 9-inch springform pan; add a layer of mousse. Place second cake layer on top; refrigerate at least 4 hours.

For mousse: In heavy saucepan over low heat, melt together chocolate chips and orange juice concentrate; cool 10 minutes. With fork, beat egg yolks well; slowly add to chocolate mixture. Mix in vanilla, sugar, and cinnamon; set aside to cool. Using electric mixer, blend cream until soft peaks form; set aside. In separate bowl, whip egg whites and salt until stiff peaks form. Fold whipped cream into cooled chocolate mixture; fold in egg whites. Do not overmix. Pour into large bowl; refrigerate. Allow mousse 2 to 3 hours to set up, and then at least 4 hours more when it is layered on cake.

For frosting: Beat together all ingredients, except garnishes. When cake and mousse layers are set, remove cake from springform pan; spread with frosting. Keep cake chilled. Garnish with sifted powdered sugar, chocolate or white chocolate shavings, or raspberry glaze.

Mousse

1 ½ cups semisweet chocolate chips
¼ cup frozen orange juice concentrate
3 eggs, separated
1 teaspoon vanilla
¼ cup sugar
Dash cinnamon
1 cup heavy cream
⅛ teaspoon salt

Frosting

6 tablespoons butter or margarine, softened
½ cup cocoa
2 cups powdered sugar, plus more for garnish
2 tablespoons milk
1 teaspoon vanilla
Powdered sugar, for garnish, optional
Chocolate or white chocolate shavings, for garnish, optional
Raspberry glaze, for garnish, optional

*Melanie Hunsaker is married to **Burke Hunsaker, BYU wide receiver in 1993.***

Sugar Cookies

Brianna Reynolds

Makes 4 to 6 dozen cookies

1 cup shortening
2 cups sugar
1 cup sour cream
1 teaspoon vanilla
3 eggs
5 cups flour
1 teaspoon salt
1 teaspoon baking soda

Buttercream Icing

Makes frosting for 2 layers or
9 x 13-inch cake or 4 to 6
dozen cookies

1 cup butter, room temperature
1 cup shortening
1 tablespoon heavy cream
½ teaspoon salt
1 teaspoon vanilla
4 cups powdered sugar

Preheat oven to 375 degrees F. Cream together shortening and sugar; add sour cream and vanilla. Beat in eggs one at a time; add remaining ingredients. Chill dough at least 2 hours; roll out to ⅛-inch thickness and cut into desired shapes. Place on greased cookie sheet; bake 8 to 10 minutes. Cool; frost with buttercream icing.

For icing: Beat together butter, shortening, cream, salt, vanilla, and 2 cups powdered sugar until smooth. Add remaining powdered sugar and beat until light and fluffy.

*Brianna Reynolds is married to **Matt Reynolds, BYU offensive lineman from 2007 to 2011.***

Melt-in-Your-Mouth Frosted Pumpkin Cookies

Kristy Denney

Makes 5 dozen cookies

Preheat oven to 350 degrees F. In large bowl, with electric mixer on medium to high speed, beat 2 cups butter 30 seconds. Beat in sugar, baking powder, baking soda, salt, cinnamon, and nutmeg until combined, scraping bowl occasionally. Add eggs and 2 teaspoons vanilla; mix in pumpkin. Add in as much flour as possible with mixer; stir in remaining flour with wooden spoon. On ungreased cookie sheet, drop dough by heaping teaspoonfuls 2 inches apart; bake 10 to 12 minutes, or until tops are set. Remove cookies to wire rack; cool. Spread cookies with frosting; if desired, sprinkle with additional cinnamon.

For frosting: In small saucepan, heat ½ cup butter and brown sugar until melted and smooth; transfer to medium bowl. Stir in milk and 1 teaspoon vanilla; beat in powdered sugar until smooth.

2½ cups butter, softened, divided
2 cups sugar
2 teaspoons baking powder
2 teaspoons baking soda
1 teaspoon salt
1 teaspoon cinnamon, plus more for garnish, optional
1 teaspoon nutmeg
2 eggs
3 teaspoons vanilla, divided
1 (15-ounce) can pumpkin
4 cups flour

Frosting
½ cup packed brown sugar
¼ cup milk
2¾ cups powdered sugar

*Kristy Denney is married to **Brett Denney, BYU defensive lineman in 2003 and from 2006 to 2009.***

the point after ▪ 93

Pumpkin Bars

Kris Anne Gustavson

Makes 64 (1-inch) bars or 32 (1 x 2-inch) bars

4 eggs
1⅔ cups sugar
1 cup oil
1 (15-ounce) can pumpkin
2 cups flour
2 teaspoons baking powder
2 teaspoons cinnamon
1 teaspoon salt
1 teaspoon baking soda
½ teaspoon nutmeg
⅓ teaspoon ground cloves
½ cup finely chopped walnuts,
   optional

Cream Cheese Icing

3 ounces cream cheese,
   softened
½ cup butter or margarine,
   softened
1 teaspoon vanilla
2 cups sifted powdered sugar

Preheat oven to 350 degrees F. Beat eggs, sugar, oil, and pumpkin until light and fluffy. Sift together flour, baking powder, cinnamon, salt, baking soda, nutmeg, and cloves; add to pumpkin mixture and mix thoroughly. Spread batter in ungreased 15 x 10-inch jelly roll pan; bake 20 to 25 minutes. Cool; frost with cream cheese icing. Sprinkle with nuts, if desired; cut into bars.

For icing: Cream together cream cheese and butter or margarine; stir in vanilla. Add powdered sugar, a little at a time, beating well until mixture is smooth.

94 ▪ the point after

*Kris Anne Gustavson is married to **Paul Gustavson, BYU center in 1973.***

Favorite Chocolate Chip Cookies

Kimberly Jacobson

Makes 2 dozen cookies

Preheat oven to 375 degrees F. In large mixing bowl, sift flour, salt, and baking soda. Beat butter, shortening, sugar, brown sugar, and vanilla extract until creamy; add eggs. Stir in flour mixture; transfer back to mixing bowl. Add chocolate chips. Drop by large spoonfuls onto ungreased baking sheet; bake 9 to 11 minutes.

2½ cups flour
1 scant teaspoon salt
1 teaspoon baking soda
½ cup butter, softened
½ cup shortening
⅔ cup sugar
⅔ cup packed brown sugar
1 teaspoon vanilla extract
2 large eggs
2 cups chocolate chips

*Kimberly Jacobson is married to **McKay Jacobson, BYU wide receiver in 2006 and from 2009 to 2011.***

The *Best* Chocolate Chip Cookies

Emily Bills

Makes 6 dozen cookies

2 cups butter, softened
1 ½ cups sugar
2 cups packed brown sugar
3 eggs
2 teaspoons vanilla
6 cups flour
1 ½ teaspoons salt
1 ½ teaspoons baking soda
4 cups semisweet chocolate
    chips

Preheat oven to 350 degrees F. Beat butter, sugar, brown sugar, eggs, and vanilla 4 minutes. Add flour, salt, and baking soda; mix until combined. Stir in chocolate chips. Drop by spoonfuls onto ungreased cookie sheet; bake 11 to 15 minutes.

*Emily Bills is married to **Kelly Bills, BYU running back from 2006 to 2007.***

Cowboy Cookies

Anna Beck Staffieri

Makes 2 dozen cookies

Preheat oven to 350 degrees F. In medium mixing bowl, combine flour, salt, baking powder, and baking soda; set aside. In large mixing bowl, cream butter and sugars; add eggs and beat until light. Add flour mixture; mix well. Stir in vanilla, rolled oats, chocolate chips, and nuts, if desired. Drop by teaspoonfuls on nonstick or greased jelly roll pan; bake 12 to 15 minutes, until edges are a golden brown.

2 cups flour

½ teaspoon salt

½ teaspoon baking powder

1 teaspoon baking soda

1 cup butter

⅔ cup packed brown sugar

½ cup sugar

2 eggs

1 teaspoon vanilla

2½ cups quick-cooking oats

1½ to 2 cups chocolate chips

1 cup chopped walnuts,
   optional

*Anna Beck Staffieri is married to **Markell Staffieri, BYU linebacker in 2001 and from 2004 to 2007;** she is also the sister of **John Beck, BYU quarterback from 2003 to 2006.***

Everything-but-the-Kitchen-Sink Cookies

Brianna Reynolds

Makes 4 to 5 dozen cookies

2 cups unsalted butter, room
    temperature

2 cups firmly packed brown
    sugar

2 cups sugar

4 large eggs

4 teaspoons vanilla extract

4 cups flour

1 tablespoon baking soda

1 ½ teaspoons salt

4 cups Rice Krispies cereal

2 cups sweetened shredded
    coconut

4 cups old-fashioned rolled oats

1 cup semisweet chocolate chips

1 cup white chocolate chips

Position rack in middle of oven; preheat oven to 350 degrees F. In large bowl, using electric mixer, cream together butter and sugars until light and fluffy. Add eggs, one at a time, beating well after each addition; beat in vanilla. Sift together flour, baking soda, and salt; beat into butter mixture to form soft dough. In separate large bowl, toss together cereal, coconut, oats, and chocolate chips. With large wooden spoon, stir dry ingredients into dough. Scoop dough into ¼-cup balls; place cookie dough balls at least 2 inches apart on parchment paper-lined baking sheets. Flatten dough balls slightly to keep cookies from puffing up too much as they bake; bake 12 to 15 minutes.

*Brianna Reynolds is married to **Matt Reynolds, BYU offensive lineman from 2007 to 2011.***

Sydney's Miniature Peanut Butter Cup Treats

Sydney Leung-Wai

Makes 3½ dozen cookies

Preheat oven to 375 degrees F. Combine butter, sugars, egg, peanut butter, and vanilla in mixing bowl; beat until smooth. In separate bowl, combine flour, baking soda, and salt; add to creamed mixture. Cover dough and chill. When cold enough to handle, gently roll dough into small balls. Place balls in ungreased mini cupcake tin; bake 8 to 9 minutes. Remove from oven; place a miniature peanut butter cup in center of each cookie.

½ cup butter, softened
½ cup packed brown sugar
½ cup sugar
1 egg
½ cup creamy peanut butter
½ teaspoon vanilla
1¼ cups flour
¾ teaspoon baking soda
½ teaspoon salt
1 (40-count) bag miniature
    Reese's peanut butter cups,
    unwrapped

*Sydney Leung-Wai is married to **Aveni Leung-Wai, BYU linebacker from 2010 to 2011.***

Lachelle's Peanut Butter Cup Cookies

Lachelle Unga

Makes 40 cookies

1¾ cups flour

½ teaspoon salt

1 teaspoon baking soda

½ cup butter, softened

½ cup sugar

½ cup peanut butter

½ cup packed brown sugar

1 egg, beaten

1 teaspoon vanilla extract

2 tablespoons milk

40 miniature chocolate-covered
  peanut butter cups,
  unwrapped

Preheat oven to 375 degrees F. Sift together flour, salt, and baking soda; set aside. Cream together butter, sugar, peanut butter, and brown sugar until fluffy. Beat in egg, vanilla, and milk; stir in dry ingredients and mix well. Shape into 40 balls; place into ungreased mini muffin pan. Bake about 8 minutes; remove from oven and immediately press a miniature peanut butter cup into each ball. Cool; carefully remove from pan.

*Lachelle Unga is married to **Uani' Unga, BYU linebacker from 2011 to 2012.***

Peanut Butter Cups

Jessica Brown

Makes 12 servings

½ cup butter
½ cup creamy peanut butter
1 cup powdered sugar
1 cup finely crushed graham
    crackers
1 cup semisweet chocolate chips

In medium microwave-safe mixing bowl, microwave butter and peanut butter together until melted; stir in powdered sugar and crushed graham crackers. Press mixture into 12 lined muffin cups. Heat and stir chocolate chips in microwave at 20-second intervals until smooth; spread on peanut butter mixture. Chill to set.

*Jessica Brown is married to **Tyrone Brown, BYU running back from 1996 to 1998.***

Peanut Butter Bars

Samantha Workman Kariya

Makes 24 bars

2½ cups graham cracker crumbs
1 cup creamy peanut butter
1 cup butter, melted
2¾ cups powdered sugar
2 cups chocolate chips

Combine all ingredients, except chocolate chips; press into ungreased 9 x 13-inch baking dish. Refrigerate 5 minutes. In microwave-safe bowl, microwave chocolate chips at medium power 1 minute; stir and heat in 30-second intervals until chocolate is melted. Spread melted chocolate over graham cracker mixture; refrigerate just until set (if chilled too long, bars are hard to cut). Cut into bars.

*Samantha Workman Kariya is married to **Bryan Kariya, BYU running back from 2008 to 2011.***

No-Bake Peanut Butter Cookies

Maddy DuPaix

Makes 21 to 24 cookies

In medium saucepan, melt butter; add sugar, salt, cocoa, and milk. Bring to a full boil; boil exactly 2 minutes. Remove from heat; add peanut butter and oats. Drop by teaspoonfuls onto waxed paper; allow to set.

Note: Use gluten-free oats, such as Bob's Red Mill Quick-Cooking Oats, for an excellent gluten-free snack.

½ cup butter

2 cups sugar

¼ teaspoon salt, optional

2 tablespoons cocoa

½ cup milk

½ cup peanut butter

2 cups quick-cooking oats

*Maddy DuPaix is the daughter of **Coach Joe DuPaix, BYU running backs coach and recruiting coordinator since 2011.***

Buffalo Chips (No-Bake Cookies)

David Coy

Makes 2 dozen cookies

2 cups sugar

½ cup milk

½ cup butter, softened

3 tablespoons cocoa

3 cups quick-cooking oats

½ cup peanut butter, creamy or
    crunchy, as desired

1 teaspoon vanilla

½ cup chopped walnuts,
    optional

In 3- or 4-quart pan, mix together sugar, milk, butter, and cocoa. Heat mixture to boiling; boil 1 minute, stirring constantly. Remove from heat; stir in remaining ingredients. Drop by spoonfuls onto waxed paper; cool and set.

Note: Cookies set as they cool. The number of servings varies depending on the size of the cookie—but there are never enough!

David Coy was a BYU wide receiver from 1981 to 1982.

Christmas Wreath Cookies

Samantha Workman Kariya

Makes 16 to 24 wreaths

Melt marshmallows and butter in a large saucepan over low heat. Remove from heat; stir in vanilla, almond extract, and food coloring. Add cornflakes; stir gently until coated. Place pan over bowl of hot water to keep mixture warm, stirring occasionally. In ¼-cup portions, place cornflake mixture on waxed paper. Quickly form portions into circles; add three red candies at the top to decorate each wreath. Cool.

32 large marshmallows
6 tablespoons butter
½ teaspoon vanilla
½ teaspoon almond extract
1 teaspoon green food coloring
4 cups cornflakes
Cinnamon decorating candies

*Samantha Workman Kariya is married to **Bryan Kariya, BYU running back from 2008 to 2011.***

Cinnamon Roll Popcorn

Christy Denney

Makes 8 servings

12 cups popped popcorn
1 cup coarsely chopped pecan
    halves
1 cup brown sugar
¾ teaspoon cinnamon
½ cup butter, cut into pieces
¼ cup light corn syrup
1 teaspoon vanilla
½ teaspoon baking soda
4 ounces almond bark

Preheat oven to 250 degrees F. In very large bowl, place popcorn and chopped pecans; set aside. In 3-quart microwave-safe bowl, combine brown sugar and cinnamon; mix well. Sprinkle butter pieces on top of sugar mixture; pour corn syrup over all. Microwave at high power 30 seconds; stir to combine. Microwave 2 minutes more; stir. Microwave 2 minutes more. Remove from microwave; stir in vanilla and baking soda (mixture will foam and rise). Pour caramel mixture over popcorn and pecans; stir until well coated. On foil-lined jelly roll pan or large cookie sheet, evenly spread popcorn mixture; bake 30 minutes, stirring every 10 minutes. Remove from oven; spread popcorn on large piece of parchment paper, waxed paper, or foil. Melt almond bark according to package instructions; drizzle over popcorn mixture. When almond bark is hardened and popcorn is cool, break into chunks.

Note: Mixture may be refrigerated to speed up cooling process.

*Christy Denney is married to **John Denney, BYU defensive end and long snapper from 2001 to 2004.***

Delectable Chocolate Almond Balls

Verna Shepherd

Makes 50 balls

Melt chopped chocolate bars; stir in whipped topping. Allow mixture to cool; shape into 1½–inch balls. Roll balls in vanilla wafer crumbs; place on tray. Chill until set; refrigerate until serving.

3 (8-ounce) milk chocolate
  almond bars, chopped
1 (8-ounce) container nondairy
  whipped topping, thawed
1 cup vanilla wafer crumbs,
  finely crushed

*Verna Shepherd is the mother of **Ed Shepherd, BYU strong safety from 1979 to 1980.***

Perfect Pie Dough

Brianna Reynolds

Makes 2 (9-inch) pie crusts

½ cup butter, softened
⅔ cup shortening
1 tablespoon sugar
½ teaspoon baking powder
1 teaspoon salt
1 tablespoon nonfat dry milk
3 cups unsifted flour
½ cup cold water

Cream together butter and shortening; add sugar, baking powder, salt, and dry milk. Add flour; mix well. Add water; mix just until blended.

Note: Crust ingredients may be combined in a mixer.

*Brianna Reynolds is married to **Matt Reynolds, BYU offensive lineman from 2007 to 2011.***

Blue and Red Berry Pie

Sara Brown

Makes 8 to 10 servings

Preheat oven to 350 degrees F. In medium saucepan, boil sugar and water until sugar is dissolved; stir in ¼ cup strawberries and cook until soft. Mash cooked berries into a sauce. Bake pie crust until it starts to brown, about 5 to 10 minutes. Mix together cream cheese and ¼ cup powdered sugar; spread cream cheese mixture onto bottom of crust. Slice remaining strawberries; combine with blueberries. Place berries in crust; cover with strawberry sauce. Bake 30 minutes. While pie is baking, in bowl combine heavy cream, 3 tablespoons powdered sugar, and vanilla; beat until soft peaks form. Remove pie from oven; cool. Before serving, top pie with whipped cream and serve with vanilla ice cream.

¼ cup sugar

¼ cup water

1 cup strawberries, divided

1 (9-inch) pie shell, unbaked

4 ounces cream cheese

¼ cup plus 3 tablespoons powdered sugar, divided

¼ cup blueberries

8 ounces heavy cream

2 teaspoons vanilla

*Sara Brown is married to **Terence Brown, BYU offensive lineman in 2005 and from 2008 to 2011.***

Whole Wheat Crust Raspberry Pie

Brooke PoVey Howell

Makes 1 (9-inch) pie

1 cup brown sugar
4 tablespoons flour
2 teaspoons quick-cooking
    tapioca
1½ tablespoons lemon juice
4 cups fresh raspberries
1 tablespoon butter, cut into
    small pieces

Pie Crust

1 cup whole wheat flour
1 cup white flour
½ cup butter
¼ cup canola oil
¼ cup water
½ teaspoon salt

Preheat oven to 450 degrees F. In small bowl, mix brown sugar, flour, tapioca, and lemon juice; sprinkle over raspberries and stir gently until well blended. Pour filling into pie crust; dot with butter. Let stand 15 minutes. Cover, if desired, with top crust or lattice pastry; bake 10 minutes. Reduce heat to 350 degrees F.; bake 40 minutes, or until crust is golden brown.

For pie crust: In medium bowl, combine whole wheat and white flours. Using pastry blender or two knives, cut butter and oil into flour; when pea-sized balls form, add water and salt. Divide dough into two pieces; roll out two crusts.

*Brooke PoVey Howell is married to **Nick Howell, BYU defensive backs coach and special team coordinator since 2008.***

Cougar Blueberry Cheesecake

Karen Slavens

Makes 15 servings

To make crust, combine graham cracker crumbs, butter or margarine, and 3 tablespoons sugar. Cover bottom of 8 x 11-inch cake pan with graham cracker crust; do not cook. Cool in refrigerator while preparing other ingredients. Mix and whip cream cheese with ⅓ cup sugar. Mix and whip powdered whipped cream mix with milk and vanilla. Blend whipped cream topping and cream cheese mixture together; pour into cake pan, evenly covering graham cracker crust. Carefully top cream cheese mixture with blueberry pie filling. Refrigerate at least one hour before serving.

1¼ cups graham cracker crumbs

⅓ cup butter or margarine

⅓ cup plus 3 tablespoons sugar, divided

1 (8-ounce) package cream cheese, softened

2 packages powdered whipped cream, such as Dream Whip

1 cup milk

1 tablespoon vanilla

2 (21-ounce) cans blueberry pie filling

*Karen Slavens is the mother of **Johnny Slavens, BYU cornerback from 1995 to 1998.***

Sweet Potato Pie

Becca Eason

Makes 8 servings

1 pound sweet potatoes
½ cup butter, softened
1 cup sugar
½ cup milk
2 eggs
½ teaspoon ground nutmeg
½ teaspoon ground cinnamon
1 teaspoon vanilla extract
1 (9-inch) unbaked pie crust

Preheat oven to 350 degrees F. Boil sweet potatoes whole in skin 40 to 50 minutes, or until tender. Run sweet potatoes under cold water; allow to cool completely. Remove skins; mash sweet potatoes in bowl. Add butter; mix well. Stir in sugar, milk, eggs, nutmeg, cinnamon, and vanilla; mix at medium speed until smooth. Pour mixture into unbaked pie crust; bake 60 minutes.

Note: Pie may puff up but will settle when cool.

*Becca Eason is married to **Corby Eason, BYU defensive back from 2009 to 2011.***

Rice Pudding

Samantha Workman Kariya

Makes 6 to 8 servings

2 cups sugar

4 cups milk

3–6 eggs, depending on size

4 cups cooked rice

Raisins, optional

Dash cinnamon

Preheat oven to 350 degrees F. Mix together sugar and milk; stir in eggs. Stir in rice; add raisins if desired. Pour into 2-quart casserole dish; sprinkle with cinnamon. Bake 1 hour; serve hot.

*Samantha Workman Kariya is married to **Bryan Kariya, BYU running back from 2008 to 2011.***

Mississippi Bread Pudding

George L. White Jr.

Makes 8 to 10 servings

1 loaf day-old French bread, cut
    into 2-inch cubes

4 cups milk

3 eggs

2 cups sugar

2 tablespoons vanilla

1 cup raisins

Rum Sauce

1 cup powdered sugar

½ cup butter

1 egg

Rum flavoring, to taste

Preheat oven to 350 degrees F., or, for glass pan, preheat to 325 degrees F. Using shortening or margarine, grease bottom of 9 x 13-inch baking pan. Soak bread in milk; crush with hands until well mixed. Add eggs, sugar, vanilla, and raisins; stir well. Bake 50 to 60 minutes, or until firm, not dry. Cool; pour warm rum sauce over pudding. Serve immediately.

For rum sauce: In top of double boiler, heat powdered sugar and butter until hot and sugar is well dissolved. In small bowl, beat egg; quickly stir in 1 to 2 tablespoons hot sugar and butter mixture to temper egg. Stir egg mixture into sugar and butter in double boiler, whipping quickly to keep egg from curdling; stir until slightly thickened. Remove from heat; add rum flavoring to taste. Store sauce in refrigerator while pudding bakes or for later use.

Note: To serve at a later time, reheat by placing broiler-safe pan under broiler long enough for sauce to bubble, approximately 1 to 2 minutes; check often. For glass pans, reheat in microwave at high power 1 to 1½ minutes.

I am from Meridian, Mississippi, and I left BYU during the Vietnam era to be a United States Navy hospital corpsman. I later married Kaylene Thornock, a BYU graduate, and for the past 35 years I have been a tenured professor at several institutions, including the University of Utah and the University of Southern Mississippi. BYU football played a great part in whatever success I have enjoyed in life. This recipe from my Mississippi roots was one of the favorites my mother made for her six sons, and I am proud to share it with other fans of BYU.

George L. White Jr. was a BYU wide receiver from 1967 to 1968.

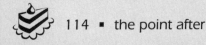

Personal Pizz-ookies

Monica DuPaix

Makes 12 servings

Chocolate chip cookie dough
Ice cream
Cookie and candy toppings,
    such as crushed Oreos,
    chopped Reese's peanut
    butter cups, shredded
    coconut, chocolate chips,
    chopped pecans, chocolate
    syrup

Preheat oven to 375 degrees F. Press thin layer of dough into bottom of 12 disposable aluminum mini loaf tins; bake 8 to 10 minutes. Remove from oven; while hot, top with scoops of ice cream and desired toppings. Serve immediately.

*Monica DuPaix is married to **Coach Joe DuPaix, BYU running backs coach and recruiting coordinator since 2011.***

Homemade Ice Cream in a Bag

Monica DuPaix

Makes 1 serving

1 (pint-sized) heavy-duty zip-top
    bag
1 tablespoon sugar
½ cup half-and-half
¼ teaspoon vanilla
1 (gallon-sized) heavy-duty zip-
    top bag
Ice
½ cup rock salt
Toppings, such as chopped or
    crushed cookies, peanut
    butter cups, sprinkles, fresh
    strawberries, nuts

In pint-sized zip-top bag, combine sugar, half-and-half, and vanilla; seal tightly. Fill gallon-sized zip-top bag half full of ice; add rock salt. Place small bag inside larger bag; seal. Shake bag until mixture thickens and turns into ice cream, 5 to 10 minutes. Take small bag out of large bag; wipe salt from top of small bag and open carefully. Add toppings; eat ice cream from the bag.

Note: For a fun activity and delicious treat, allow children to make individual servings of ice cream in a bag.

*Monica DuPaix is married to **Coach Joe DuPaix, BYU running backs coach and recruiting coordinator since 2011.***

He-Man Milk Toast

Vern Swanson

Makes 1 serving

1 (16-ounce) glass milk
2 slices bread
Butter, to taste
Jam or jelly, to taste

Fill drinking glass about ⅓ full of milk. Toast 2 slices bread to desired doneness; while toast is still hot, spread with butter and jam or jelly. Place toast slices together to form a sandwich; fold sandwich in half lengthwise. Stuff sandwich into glass of milk; eat with a spoon.

When I played football under Tommy Hudspeth from 1964 to 1967, several of the team members had toasters and small refrigerators in their rooms in the football dorm (Helaman Halls' John Hall). About 10 or 11 p.m., all the guys would be hungry and want a snack—and the He-Man Milk Toast recipe was invented! No sophisticated dish will ever replace this team favorite in the hearts and minds of all the "third floor John Hall Animals," as we were called. The pièce de résistance, of course, is when the sandwich is plunged into the glass of milk! Mmm, good! This dish is guaranteed to make you sleep at night and run faster during practice. We still believe it was the key to the Cougars winning their first football title in 1965.

Vern Swanson was a BYU running back from 1964 to 1967.

Delicious Limeade

Brianna Reynolds

Makes 8 servings

4 limes
⅓ cup sweetened condensed
    milk
1 cup sugar, divided
6 cups water, divided

Combine whole limes, sweetened condensed milk, ½ cup sugar, and 3 cups water in blender; pulse just until pulp is blended. Strain into a pitcher; add remaining 3 cups water and up to ½ cup sugar to taste. Serve with plenty of ice.

*Brianna Reynolds is married to **Matt Reynolds, BYU offensive lineman from 2007 to 2011.***

Grape Sparkle

Verna Shepherd

Makes 3 quarts or 12 servings

2 cups sugar
4 cups water
2 cups orange juice
2 cups grape juice
Juice of 2 lemons
1 (2-liter) bottle lemon-lime soda
   or ginger ale

In large pot over low heat, stir sugar and water until sugar is dissolved; cool. Stir in orange juice, grape juice, and lemon juice. Pour into a freezer-safe container; freeze several hours, occasionally chopping mixture into slushy consistency. To serve, spoon slush into individual cups; pour lemon–lime soda or ginger ale over slush.

*Verna Shepherd is the mother of **Ed Shepherd, BYU strong safety from 1979 to 1980.***

Lemon Slush

Verna Shepherd

Makes 3 quarts or 12 servings

2 cups sugar

2 quarts water

1 (12-ounce) can frozen
    lemonade concentrate

1 (2-liter) bottle lemon-lime soda
    or ginger ale

In large pot over low heat, stir sugar and water until sugar is dissolved; stir in lemonade concentrate. Pour into a freezer-safe container; freeze several hours, occasionally chopping mixture into slushy consistency. To serve, spoon into individual cups; pour soda or ginger ale over slush.

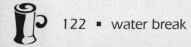

*Verna Shepherd is the mother of **Ed Shepherd, BYU strong safety from 1979 to 1980.***

Muscle Recovery Smoothie

Mary Jolley

Makes 1 large smoothie

1 small banana, sliced
1 pear, sliced
2 cups baby spinach leaves
2 teaspoons flaxseed
¼ cup cold water
½ cup frozen cherries
½ cup frozen blueberries
½ cup crushed ice

Layer ingredients in blender in order listed; process until well blended.

Note: Greens, fruit, and flaxseeds supply a quick boost of vitamins, minerals, protein, and omega-3s to replenish and strengthen muscles after exercise.

*Mary Jolley is married to **Doug Jolley, BYU tight end from 1997 to 2001.***

On-the-Go Green Smoothie

Brooke PoVey Howell

Makes 4 servings

1–2 cups fresh spinach
1 ripe mango, peeled and
    coarsely chopped
2 cups orange juice
2–4 cups frozen raspberries or
    blueberries
Splenda, if sweetening is
    needed, optional
½ cup ice, optional

Place all ingredients in high-speed blender; process until smooth. Serve immediately.

*Brooke PoVey Howell is married to **Nick Howell, BYU defensive backs coach and special team coordinator since 2008.***

Sore Throat Soother

Sara Brown

Makes 2 (4-ounce) servings

2 tablespoons honey
8 ounces water
1 large lemon
Pinch cayenne pepper

Pour honey into bottom of heat-resistant cup. Boil water and pour over honey; mix well. Juice ½ lemon and slice other half. Add juice and a few lemon slices to hot water and honey mixture; add cayenne pepper to taste.

*Sara Brown is married to **Terence Brown, BYU offensive lineman in 2005 and from 2008 to 2011.***

Index